Neville Goddard.

The Frank Carter Lectures

Audio Enlightenment Press

Giving Voice to the Wisdom of the Ages

Printed in the United States of America

0 1 2 3 4 5 6 7 8 9

ISBN 978-1-941489-37-6

www.AudioEnlightenmentPress.com

www.MetaPhysicalPocketBooks.Com

First Printing April 2018

The Frank Carter Lectures

Preface		1
Forward		3
Chapter 1	Neville, The Law, The Promise, and Frank	5
Chapter 2	"The Hidden Secret of GOD, Neville Goddard"	9
Chapter 3	"Bear Ye One Another's Burdens, Neville Goddard"	25
Lecture 1		37
Lecture 2		45
Lecture 3		57
Lecture 4		67
Lecture 5		79
Lecture 6		93
Lecture 7		105
Lecture 8		119
Lecture 9		127
Lecture 10		139
Lecture 11		151
Summary		161
Free Metaphysical Resources		163

Publishers Preface

I have been researching and publishing the works of the great mystic Neville Goddard for over 7 years now and it is a never ending quest trying to locate lost lectures and gems of wisdom that Neville left behind for humanity. We are fortunate in the sense that most metaphysical authors and scholars of his era left very little behind in regard to lectures or audios. With Neville, we are blessed with an abundance of gold.

My search has proved fruitful on many occasions. One of the nuggets of gold that I uncovered was a series of lectures that his friend and chauffer Frank Carter left behind. After Neville's death, Frank did a series of 12 lectures over a period of 6 months. All but one of them was salvageable, and we have transcribed and assembled the eleven lectures, with two lectures from Neville that are particularly pertinent to Franks lectures. As with all transcriptions from poor quality recordings, we did our best to preserve the text. I have included a link at the back of the book to the audios for those that have questions in regard to the transcriptions.

There are many people and students that have embraced Neville's teachings worldwide, but none that I am aware of that are as knowledgeable as Liz Baker. I have known Liz for over 5 years and her grasp of Neville's teachings is unsurpassed, which is why I asked her to write the forward, the first chapter and the summary of this book.

There is much truth and wisdom in these lectures and we are glad to have them in circulation once again. As always, it is my great pleasure to bring lost wisdom to the students of Neville and the World.

Barry J Peterson
Publisher

Foreword

Frank Carter, friend of Neville Goddard (1905-1972) the twentieth century Christian Mystic, Author and Lecturer, gave a series of lectures in 1976, concerning his belief by way of his own vision and knowledge of scriptural meaning, that Neville Goddard's death had fulfilled scripture. The lectures contained in this book may not include every single lecture in Frank's series, and some of the audio was poor quality for transcription, but what we do have reveals little known details about Neville, a few anecdotes, Neville's last written words, and most importantly reveals what Neville's death meant scripturally, for us all.

This book is not meant to be an exhaustive tale of Neville's life or even his work. In fact, the lectures, given by Frank Carter are focused more on Neville's last days and night, and Franks subsequent visions and understanding that Neville himself appeared in scripture. Neville's work is growing in popularity on the internet with available audio recordings and written lectures that continue to emerge, not to mention his books and booklets that can be purchased easily now. As more and more people come to find Neville's work, typically by way of learning The Law that Neville taught, I hope they continue to study Neville long enough to find truth mirrored back to them, to find themselves in Neville's work. As he said, the whole story in The Bible is actually about us, about awakening.

This book of lectures can appeal to any truth seeker, or Bible lover, and especially any student of Neville Goddards who has read and believed. Grab a Bible and a concordance and follow along as Frank shares what he has found. The lectures contained in this book, in Franks words, are intended to reveal the great revealer. Frank said of Neville... "This man stepped out of the pages of scripture and came to us and gave us the great secret, and told us whatever we do, don't worship him. Don't make him into a demigod, this is all for awakening. "

I would like to thank Barry Peterson, for allowing me to be a part of introducing these lectures. Barry's passion for sharing truth and enlightenment, has blessed my life more than words can say. I feel blessed to be a part of this project, as I have a true love, respect and gratitude for Neville's work. Franks lectures have touched my heart, and my spirit said Amen, Amen and Amen! To the truth contained within them.

Liz Baker

Chapter 1

Neville, The Law, The Promise, and Frank

"The man who has experienced scripture cannot escape telling it's meaning to his fellow men"

Neville –Resurrection

Neville Goddard was a 20th century Author, Lecturer and Christian Mystic who began teaching in 1938, the use and origin of what he called The Law, how to use ones imagination, to create what you want in this world. In his first book Your Faith is your Fortune Neville said "I AM that in which all my conceptions of myself live and move and have their being, and apart from which they are not. I dwell within every conception of myself; from this withinness, I ever seek to transcend all conceptions of myself. By the very law of my being, I transcend my conceptions of myself, only as I believe myself to be that which does transcend. I AM the law of being and beside ME there is no law.

I AM that I AM." Neville taught the principle of the law of being, also called the law of assumption or consciousness..in practical ways. Neville was fond of saying, that which is most profoundly spiritual is most directly practical. And insisted that if we but believe that the indwelling spirit of man is the source of all life, and saying yes to everything we think, picture and emotionalize, that there is nothing that man cannot achieve if we use this law to consciously create what we want by imagining that we have it now. Neville went on to teach the use of imagination to pray for others, to heal relationships, to gain promotion in ones own life and achieve goals that formerly seemed out of reach. There are numerous good reports and examples in Neville's work of the many ways his students used the law for their own benefit and, for the benefit of others.

In another quote, from the first chapter of Your Faith is Your Fortune, it is obvious that this was the beginning of Neville's journey in revealing the mysteries of the bible and this would be the course he remained on for the rest of his life...revelation of truth hidden in plain sight, in the bestselling book of all time, the most read book of all time, the most studied book of all time, The Bible, yet few understand... "This Lord God, creator of heaven and earth, is discovered to be man's awareness of being. If man was less bound by orthodoxy and more intuitively observant he could not fail to notice in the reading of the Bibles that the awareness of being is revealed hundreds of times throughout this literature. To name a few I AM hath sent me unto you. Be still and know that I AM God I AM the Lord and there is no God... I AM the shepherd. I AM the door. I AM the resurrection and the life. I AM the way. I AM the beginning and the end." (pg. 438 in Neville Goddard: The Complete Reader)

By his own account, Neville studied the bible for 8 hours a day for decades and spent much time meditating upon the word. Neville lectured multiple times weekly with no notes in hand, up until the time of his death in 1972, and could quote from multiple versions of the bible at will, from memory, on the platform. Neville was invited to take part on late night television discussion forums; he spoke on the radio, and made two albums of his lectures. This was only the beginning of a long career of Neville teaching the mysteries of the bible, the beginning of revealing layer upon layer of deeper meaning in the Bible than anyone has, before or since his time.

Neville had become a popular teacher of The Law, first in NYC and later in Los Angeles and San Francisco, drawing crowds of thousands for many years. After experiencing a series of visions, from 1959 to 1963, that he called The Promise, Neville explained that it had been revealed to him in those visions that he was the father of David.. God the Father, in the act of awakening. Furthermore, Neville revealed that this is the story of every man, that we are all truly one, but individual expressions of the one God and that every man will be awakened individually in their own time, by way of vision, that we live in a world of shadows and symbols and our only purpose here is to awaken to the being that we truly are, thus expanding in love. This was Neville's awakening, the most thorough account of these visions are recorded in his final book, Resurrection. Neville revealed that he had been called to teach the true meaning of scripture, to tell this story, his story, and to reveal the mystery of scripture, to anyone who would listen and from that moment on he simply taught those who were drawn to him, and the crowds subsequently dwindled. Those who remained, he said, were the ones who could believe his teachings on faith, it is many of those faithful students who kept recordings, and transcribed many of the lectures that we have available for us to enjoy today. Many of Neville's followers were experiencing visions of their own at this time and Neville loved to share their stories and letters from the platform and describe in detail the symbolism that the visions contained.

Frank Carter, attended his lectures for more than three years and became a friend and student of Neville's. There are audios of Neville lecturing where you can hear Neville call for Frank to come up at the end of the lecture to speak to him. Frank would drive him to and from his speaking engagements and to run other errands when Neville's usual driver, a man named David Morton, could not. It is clear that Frank and Neville developed a loving and trusted friendship and that Frank was a devoted student of Neville's and The Bible. It was Frank Carter who spent Neville's last day with him and was the last person to see him alive. Not much is known as of now about Frank, other than the few details he reveals in his own lectures, but the love and admiration that he had for Neville and his wife, is apparent, as is the tremendous amount of respect he had for Neville's work. Frank admits he had believed whole heartedly that what Neville taught was true, with little personal reason to believe other than a vision he had several years before Neville's passing, and, faith. Franks experiences with Neville may bring tears to your eyes as he discusses his last days, and then reveals to you the reader, that Neville

7

Goddard is indeed in the bible, in fact all over the Bible, unlike books of the bible given a name about the main character... The revelation of Neville can be found all throughout scripture, thanks to Frank's diligent work, his own visions, study and his lectures shared within this book. . Frank mentions that Neville was referring to him in a particular lecture, concerning a very important vision that he had of Neville; the following two chapters are simply two Neville lectures which are the perfect lead in to Franks lectures.

Liz Baker

Chapter 2

Neville (04-12-1971)

THE HIDDEN SECRET OF GOD

The mysteries of God are mysterious in character, yet they are proclaimed to all who can understand them. Paul, in his letter to the Corinthians – the first letter, you read this in the 2nd chapter of I Corinthians. He is telling them a story that their faith may not rest in the wisdom of men, but in the power of God. Now, he speaks of a different wisdom altogether.

He said: "Yet, among the mature, we teach wisdom. It is not a wisdom of this age or of the rulers of this age, for they are all doomed to pass away." (I Corinthians 2:6) He speaks of an entirely different wisdom that he claims to be the secret – "the hidden secret of God, which God decreed before the ages for our glorification." (I Corinthians 2:7) Then he said: "For what person knows the thoughts of a man except the spirit of the man which dwells in him? So also, no one comprehends the thoughts of god except the Spirit of God." (I Corinthians 2:11)

Now we are told, after the Resurrection those who were closest to him still did not understand him. For when He appeared, they said, "Lord, will you now, at this time, restore the kingdom to Israel?"

And He said to them, "It is not for you to know times and seasons which the Father has fixed by His own authority. But you wait until you receive the power which will come upon you when the Holy Spirit comes upon you."

That is the power of which I speak, when the Holy Spirit comes upon you. And then, with that power, you will be my witnesses, witnessing in Jerusalem and in all Judea and Samaria to the ends of the earth, but not until it comes upon you, and when it comes upon you, you are told, the

Holy Spirit is one's remembrance. "He will bring to your remembrance all things that I have told you." The whole will come back, and then you will actually reproduce within yourself my story – that's what He is telling them.

He now disappears. He has now revealed to them the true Exodus, that the Exodus of the Old Testament was an adumbration – a foreshadowing. Resurrection followed by the *birth from above* is the true *Exodus* from this world of tears, this world of bondage. So, the Jews celebrate the Exodus, and they are still in bondage, and the Christians celebrate the Resurrection, and they haven't yet been resurrected. That whole thing is a drama.

When the Spirit comes upon you, which is the spirit of power, then "he will bring to your remembrance all that I have told you, which I have received from my Father." So, within the individual upon whom this power comes, which is the Holy Spirit, the whole thing will unfold within him.

They completely misunderstood it, and they thought the restoration of a national theocracy was what was intended with the coming of Messiah. They did not realize that the truest coming of Jesus was the manifest power of the Holy Spirit, that when this power comes, it lifts you up from within yourself, and then you actually are the Being that the world yesterday celebrated about his Resurrection. *You* are that One spoken of in Scripture. But you will not *know* it and be a witness to this until the power comes upon you. And that power is the power of the Holy Spirit. Then the whole thing unfolds within you.

Now, you have heard of the story – you all know the story. Did you ever dwell upon the character called "Judas"? Today we speak of a man who is a betrayer of a trust – he is a *Judas*. He simply betrayed the trust – any kind of a trust. A man just died in New York City in prison who betrayed the trust of the Mafia.[1] He was one of the leaders in the Mafia, and he gave to the FBI the true name, "Our Thing" – Cosa Nostra. No one claimed his body. There he was, he died in prison because there was a price on his head – a fabulous price to kill him. So, he was protected while he was in prison because he had revealed the secret of this thing that wormed its way into society called "Our Thing," where they made billions that you could not put a finger on it; therefore it wasn't taxable. But he betrayed it; so he was a *Judas*.

Well, that is not the Judas of Scripture. But who is this Judas? We are told that at the Last Supper he said, "The one to whom I will give the sop, for my time has come" – everything was done on order in the Gospel of John. He never moved. He resisted all action until the right moment. "My time has not yet come," beginning with the second chapter. He said to the brothers in the seventh chapter, "My hour has not yet come." He goes through the entire book stating that the time has not yet come; he is following a divine plan.

So here we find predestination in one, and we find free will both joined together in man. He teaches man to exercise free will, and shows them how to change the pattern of life, but *he* is under compulsion to fulfill the Father's will. Everything must be done on time. So, the moment of betrayal has come.

In the Oriental custom, two would sit on a divan or couch. The honored guest was always the one to whom the host gave the sop. He would take the sop, dip it into the dish, and then hand it to the honored guest. So, "The one to whom I give it, *he* will betray me." He turns and gives it to Judas, and Judas goes out quickly; and he said to him, "What you have to do, do quickly." It is perfectly told, may I tell you, I know from experience. "What you have to do, do quickly." And Judas goes out.

---

[1] Joseph M. Valachi died 3 April 1971, at age 67, having disclosed the workings of Cosa Nostra to 1963 Senate.

Yet they do not understand who it is going to be who will betray him.

"Lord, is it I?"

"Lord, is it I?"

"Lord, is it I?"

Well, it is obvious the one to whom he gave it. Who, then, is Judas? He betrays the Messianic secret. Now, "No one knows the thoughts of God, but the Spirit of God." Is he not, then, the Spirit of God? If he betrays God, only the Spirit of God could betray God, "for no man knows the thoughts of a man but the spirit of man, which dwells in him, and no one knows or comprehends the thoughts of God but the Spirit of God." Then, is he not the Spirit of God? For, no one can betray me but the spirit of myself!

Now we are told there are two traditions as to his *death* in Scripture. Matthew tells it in the 27th chapter that he went out and hanged himself. In other words, he committed suicide. Jesus is made to say, "No one takes away my life. I lay it down myself. I have the power to lay it down and the power to take it up again." So, here we find the suicide – the parallel. But in the book of Acts, it is said, "He swelled up, and swelling up, he burst in the middle. Then all of his bowels came gushing out." (Acts 2:28) They were two entirely different traditions: one given us by Luke, for Luke wrote the book of Acts; and then we have the one in Matthew.

Now a friend of mine – and he is here tonight – he said, "This happened to me a year ago. I didn't tell it because I didn't know – it seemed so strange to me. But this weekend I was reading the 13th chapter of the book of John, reading of the Last Supper, reading all about the sop – reading of these things, and I wondered, 'What nonsense! They saw where he gave the sop – to whom he gave it. Why ask all these questions? Is it I? Is it I? And then one whispered to ask him who it is.'

"The honored guest could not be across the street, the honored guest

12

would be right next to him – the one whose head was on his bosom, and he dipped the sop and gave him, and said, 'What you have to do, do quickly.'"

Now he said, "A year ago I had a vision, and in my vision I saw you dead. You were dead. You were dressed in white – radiant white, and your bowels were completely out. That was your death. Not understanding it, I hesitated to mention it because it struck me at the time that that would be Judas. And so, I saw you dressed in white – radiant white, and you were dead, and your death was caused by the swelling up and the bursting in your middle, and out came all of your bowels, gushing out."

Here was Neville, and he was dead. He saw the perfect vision. I tell you, when it happens everything in you, "All you behold, though it *appears* without, it is within, in your own wonderful human imagination, of which this world of mortality is but a shadow." [Blake, from "Jerusalem"]

So, all these characters are within himself! And the nearest to him is the *Spirit* of himself, which is Judas. The word *Judas* is the same as *Judah* – the one mentioned in the genealogy. And speak – of the genealogy, "Jacob [was] the father of Judah and his brothers." (Matthew 1:2) It didn't mention the first three brothers. It never mentioned the first three; it jumps over the first three and goes to the fourth one, Judah. *Judah* means the *hand*, but it's the hand of God, the *power* of God. It's the creative power of God, the directive power of God that can fulfill His purpose. And *His purpose is to give Himself to man.*

The story of Jesus is the biography of God. That's God. Now, when that unfolds itself in man, God has succeeded in *giving* Himself to man – *That* man then tells it.

So, today here we single out an individual as though this thing happened on earth. It didn't happen on earth. This is God's plan. It is all written in Scripture. When it happens in you, you read Scripture to find the parallel, but the whole thing is taking place in a supernatural world – all within you. "He speaks to man through the medium of dreams, but He *reveals* Himself in vision." It is God unveiling Himself.

So, one who comes into my world – and no one comes unless the Father within me calls him – he has a vision. He hesitated for quite a while to tell me because of the tradition concerning Judas. He was the one whose bowels, as he swelled up he burst in the middle, and all of his bowels gushed out. He was the one who betrayed the secret, as I betray it every time I take this platform. I am telling you the *secret* of God every time I take this platform. I am playing the part of Judas every Monday and Friday night. I play it every time I talk to a friend. If they call me on the phone, I am betraying the secret. "I have come, not to abolish the law and the prophets, but to fulfill them." So, I tell you the Law. I reinterpret the Law psychologically, and tell you that, "An assumption, though false, if persisted in will harden into fact." [Sir Anthony Eden]

Two thousand years ago you heard that same statement told in this manner, "Whatever you desire, *believe* that you have received it, and you will." It's the identical thing told in a more modern form – the same thing. If you dare to assume this, that or the other, and persist in your assumption, it will harden into fact and project itself on the screen of space. That is the Law. It's psychological.

Now the Prophets – they predicted the sufferings of the coming One, and told of the glory that would be His. First, He was chosen in Him before the foundation of the world. "Those whom He *foreknew*, He also predestined to be conformed to the image of His Son; and those whom He *predestined*, He also called, and those whom He *called* He also justified, and those whom He *justified* He also *glorified*."

Well, you can't take these five terms and come to any other conclusion than predestination. That is the Spirit-in-man fulfilling the Will of God, leading that man up to God Himself! For the story of the

14

Gospel is *God's* biography. When that story unfolds itself in the individual in the first-person-singular and present tense experience, now it's *his* biography, and if it's God's biography and it is his experience, then who is he? He *is* that Power. When that power comes upon him, he is power. And who is the power of God? Jesus Christ. "Christ the power of God and the wisdom of God."

When someone, now, puts his or her hand to the plow and turning back, he unfits himself for the Kingdom of Heaven, but the One Who called him will not allow him, or allow her, to unfit himself, or herself, for that Kingdom. And so, if he appears to her or to him as sheer power, it is for a purpose.

As we are told, "If one will not believe, having been called and having been spoken to," as told us in the story of Gabriel (Luke 1:18-23), "And Gabriel came into the presence of Zechariah and told Zechariah that the Lord had sent him," and then told Zechariah of the coming of the birth of John, and he said, "How will I know this? I am an old man, and my wife is advanced in years." And the Angel replied, "I am Gabriel. I stand in the presence of God" – that is, wherever the messenger is sent, God is with him, for the Sender and the *sent* are one. And the word *Gabriel* means either the *power* of God or the *man* of God. You can translate it in either way.

So, now you want a sign? "Well, this shall be your sign: you shall be silent and unable to speak until that day when this thing is fulfilled." And when he came out of the Temple, he could not speak, and those who waited on the outside in prayer while he lit the incense on the inside were dumbfounded because they knew something had happened when they saw him. He couldn't speak; he was dumb."

Then, when the child was born, and then on the 8th day, which was the day now to be circumcised, they wanted to know what to name the child; and they thought certainly *Zechariah*, after his father. And he made signs, for he could not speak, to bring him a tablet, that he could write, and he wrote on the tablet, "His name is John."[2] And as he wrote, "His name is John," the whole thing was fulfilled, his mouth was opened, his tongue was loosed, and then he spoke. That was sheer power. "Christ is the power of God and the wisdom of God." But in this world of ours, when I am put into the place of playing such a part, in His infinite mercy He takes from my conscious, reasoning mind that individual act that I am not left with it, that I will play in the depths of my own being – I will play anything that my Father, who is one with my Self, commands me to play, that they who would now stray from the path will be brought back into it.

If that little thing was only for one moment that you are dumb, unable to speak – and here for one moment there was no speech, but I tell you, this play is the Eternal Play. It didn't close yesterday when the Bowl overflowed and all of a sudden they came out, when they reinterpreted the entire story and called it "positive thinking" or "positive decisions" and all this nonsense. This is the *eternal* story.

Wait until you receive power from on high, for the power will come and you will be overcome with the Spirit – the Holy Spirit, and "when the Holy Spirit comes upon you, it will bring to your remembrance all that I have told you." And what have I told you? My life. I have told you exactly what happened to me supernaturally. That will then happen to you individually, and you will know that I told you the truth. That is the *eternal* story of the Gospel.

So when he said, "Among the mature, I too impart a wisdom, it is not the wisdom of this age or of the rulers of this age, for they are doomed to pass away. I impart a secret and hidden wisdom of God which God decreed before the ages for our glorification."

That's what he imparted. Then he tells us in that same chapter, the 2nd chapter of I Corinthians, how it's impossible for any person to know

---

[2] John the Baptist

a man's thoughts, except the spirit of that man which dwells in him, and therefore no one knows or comprehends the thoughts of God except the Spirit of God.

And so, He sends the Spirit upon you. So the real coming of Jesus – the return of Jesus, in the truest sense, is simply the manifested power of the Holy Spirit. That's his *coming*. He can't come in any other way. He becomes invisible. He departs this world, and then sends the Holy Spirit. Well, the Holy Spirit comes like the wind, may I tell you – just like the wind! And when you hear it, it's the most unearthly sound you have ever heard, but it's *wind*. It possesses you, and then you wake. And you wake to find yourself entombed, and then you come out of that tomb where you have been buried, and then everything – the entire story now – unfolds within you, scene after scene without any deviation, and that's the Being that you are. And when it happens and it comes to the very end, you know Who-You-Are. You are God Himself!

You are the Power of God that is Jesus Christ – "the power of God and the wisdom of God." And now you know the true Exodus from bondage. What you read about in the Old Testament was only an adumbration – a foreshadowing, but when it happens to you, this is the true Exodus when you are set free – set free because you have found the Son. "If the Son sets you free, you are free indeed." And the Son stands before you, and you know exactly who he is, and he knows who you are.

So, don't close the book and wait for a year. "Set your hope fully upon the Grace that is coming to you at the unveiling and the revelation of Christ in you." For that's where He is! He is all buried within you.

In the meanwhile, use the Law psychologically. External observation means nothing. All the outside ceremonies mean nothing – absolutely nothing. It's all just – well, that was my command when I was *sent*: "Down with the bluebloods" – all church protocol. That's what it means. Down with it completely. Pay no attention to it – even to the little simple thing, which is a very pleasant thing: When you sit down to dine and someone calls upon you to say grace, say grace. Don't be abusive about it, say it, but you know it means nothing. But do it if you are called upon to do it. We do not have it at home. We sit down and I thoroughly enjoy my meal that my wife prepared, and I thank *her* for preparing it. But if one calls upon you to do it, do it, but all outside ceremony means absolutely nothing. That was my command when I was *sent*: "Down with the bluebloods" – down with all church protocol.

So, the so-called "kissing of the feet"[3] that you saw in this picture the other day and the washing of the feet of these twelve elderly men and kissing the feet – that's out! It hasn't a thing to do with real, real Christianity.

I tell you what it is from experience. He will wake within you, and then you will know every one of those Disciples – what aspect of your own being each represents. And that one who was closest to him, the one who was his friend, the one to whom he gave the honored piece – that was Judas, the *Hand* of God – the directive hand that could fulfill his purposed end by *betraying* the secret, as I do every time I talk to you. I *betray* the secret of God. I can't betray it if I don't know it. No one can betray what he does not know, and so one must first know it to betray it. But I am betraying it. I am telling you exactly how it happens. It happens in the way that I have told you.

It will come suddenly upon you – the Holy Spirit. It will come like a storm wind, and when it comes, you will wake to find yourself entombed, and then you will have the innate wisdom – for Christ is also the wisdom of God, not only the power of God – to move that stone from where it was. That was the *seal*. Break it by pushing it from within, and you will come out, and you will find surrounding you the witnesses to the Great Event that God succeeded in His purpose, which was *waking you as God*. For this is the *birth* of God, "not born of blood or of the will of the flesh

---

[3] "The Shoes of the Fisherman" by Morris West

or the will of man, but of God." And you come out, and the sign of your *birth* is present, and here is the *sign* wrapped – as you are told – in swaddling clothes. And you pick it up and in the most endearing manner you say, "How is my sweetheart?" and the whole thing vanishes, including the three witnesses who witnessed the birth.

Then comes the second Great Event, when he stands before you, and you fulfill Scripture, the 89th Psalm: "I have found David, and he has cried unto me, 'Thou art my Father, my God, and the Rock of my Salvation.'" And then he stands before you. And this relationship is forever. It's the returning memory, for you do not have the feeling that it happens now. It's simply that your memory has returned, just as though you had suffered from total amnesia.

It's not something that startles you; you have *always known* he was your *son.*

That's the feeling that I had. So, all of a sudden, he comes back. *What* comes back? Well, "the Holy Spirit is upon me." Well, *who* is the Holy Spirit? He "who brings to your remembrance all that I have told you."

"And did not David, in the spirit, call me 'my Lord'?" Well, when he calls you "my lord" – which is the name of my Father, for all sons called their father and spoke of their father as "my lord" – so, "David, in the spirit, called me 'my lord.'" He does it *in spirit*, not here on earth.

And then comes the grand severance of your body from top to bottom, and your ascent into heaven, separating the event called "Resurrection" from the "Ascension." And you can count them. It's not any forty days. You can count the whole thing up. It's between – mine was on the 20th of July of '59, and, the Ascent took place on the 8th day of April of 1960, and that's when one ascends – ascends into Heaven. And the whole thing, as you are told, reverberates like thunder.

And then comes the Seal of Approval on the twelve hundred and sixtieth day. And that is the descent of the Holy Spirit in bodily form as a dove. And here he rests upon you. You bring him up, and he is smothering you with kisses when the whole thing fades. And then you come, and you tell it.

And so, the story of Judas – when he does betray, he does it quickly, I tell you. You are seated on the floor explaining the Word of God to those who are seated before you, and he is one of them. And suddenly he jumps up, and you know exactly what he is going to do. He is going to tell – you don't use the word *betray* – he is going to tell exactly what he heard *you* say, you are speaking of the Kingdom of God. And he is going to tell that you are speaking of the Kingdom, and that you are the King, and he is going to tell the authorities concerning what you said. He has to betray the Kingdom, and he goes out and he tells it.

Then comes the *authority* in, and he unveils your arm, and his name who went out is the "Arm of God," the "Hand of God." He unveils it, and you see the relationship between the one who went out and yourself. Now you are completely unveiled when he nails into your shoulder that peg – that wooden peg and hammers it in, and then takes off the sleeve and takes the arm and it's bare. And then you know the 53rd chapter of Isaiah, "Who has believed our report, and to whom has the Arm of the Lord been revealed?" And as everything is placed upon that Being, he has then to bear the burden, but he will see the travail of his efforts – of his labour, and he will rejoice. He will be satisfied when he knows that he got through.

So, you can say to any one, if they see me in any role that seems a harsh role, then know that I consciously am not aware of it while I played that part. I have to play it, for this is a supernatural world of which I speak, it is a supernatural Being of which I speak, it's a supernatural part that I am playing when I play those parts at night. And certain parts, I am relieved of the memory of them, for they have to be done – to "jack one up" – "having put his hand to the plow and turning back, unfits himself for the Kingdom of Heaven." (Luke 9:62)

And what caused him to turn back? *Doubt.*

They questioned, and so when Zechariah said, "How will I know this? I am an old man, and my wife is advanced in years. How could she conceive and bear a son?" he said, "I stand in the presence of God." In other words, I am speaking for the One who sent me, and He never left me. Therefore he stands with me. Now sheer power is going to make you dumb, and so he said to him, "You will be silent, unable to speak, until that which I have foretold has come to pass, because you did not believe the words that He gave me to speak. I spoke them, but you did not believe my words."

So, you will see me in many roles. Many of you have seen me in different roles. Yet my conscious, reasoning mind has always been removed on my return from certain parts that I had to play, for I am under compulsion to play those parts, after being awakened. And my friend had to see me in that role to know who Judas really is. And I am Judas every time I betray the Messianic secret. And I am the one who told him to do it quickly.

That scene I recall vividly. "What you have to do, do quickly." He certainly did it quickly. There was no time between his departure and the arrival of the authority who came in and severed my sleeve and hammered into my shoulder that wooden peg, on which he then placed the burden.

So, I tell you, this play is an eternal play. It goes on forever and forever and forever, and each one makes his exit – which is the Exodus – from this world of tears into a blissful state, but only in that way does he ever make the Exodus. So when they sing the hymns of how they were led out of bondage in Egypt into a world of freedom – and yet all are still as enslaved as they were thousands of years ago, then what are they commemorating? For when the real leader – the new Moses – comes;

21

they would not recognize him.

The new Moses came and was called "Jesus," which means *Jehovah*. God Himself came this time in the form of man. And that's the new Moses, and his life is the pattern that man will one day imitate – actually experience, and therefore, it's *his* pattern. It is his, and it's the only way you will ever make an exit from this world. *Death* will not take you out of this world. You will *die* and be restored to life just as you are now, in a world just like this. It's terrestrial, and you will still be making your effort as you do it right now.

There is no transforming power whatsoever in the thing called *death*. There is no transformation in death. You find yourself the same being. Young, yes, but that's not transformation – the same identity. But that of which I speak is a complete transfiguration – a complete transformation of form. You are no longer this little garment. You are glorified, and you *wear* a glorified Body that doesn't have the needs of this body at all. And wherever you go clothed in that Body, everything is perfect. There is no place you could go. Walk through *hell*; it will become heaven. And someone clothed in *these* garments [indicating the physical body], walking through heaven, would turn it into *hell*.

So, I tell you, you are in for the most glorious thing in the world. And what I have told you, I tell you from my own personal experience. I am not theorizing, I am not speculating; I knew that someone had to see me in that role, and he had this vision a year ago, but because of custom and his association with the idea of Judas as the one whose bowels – first of all, he swelled up, and swelling up he burst in the middle, and all of his bowels came gushing out.

And loving me as he does, and believing me as he does, he didn't know how to associate that with the one that he so loves and trusts to tell the truth. Well, I can tell you, they are the same being, for he is the spirit of the one – the honored guest to whom he gave the sop. That is the honored position, not around a table as we have it here in da Vinci's

22

picture. There was no table, not in the Oriental world. You sat on a divan – not more than two at any one moment, and divans were around. And the host, if he ever dipped it, would take a piece of meat and dip it, and the one to whom he gave the meat or piece of bread – that was the sop – the one to whom he gave it, that was the honored guest. As we today, sitting around the table, we seat the honored guest to our right, and here that is the honored position. But there, the one whose head was on his breast – and he just simply said, "Who is it?" Who is nearest to you but your spirit? "So, no one knows or comprehends the thoughts of God but the Spirit of God."

So, if God was ever betrayed, He could only be betrayed by the Spirit of God. It had to be revealed. It could not be discovered by any philosophical reasoning. No man in this world, as you are told in Scripture – "Man could not find God." All the wisdom of man could not find God. God had to reveal Himself, and the revealing is the betrayal of God. He betrays Himself by unveiling Himself to man. And this is the story as it is written and told us in Scripture.

You set your hope fully upon that moment in time when it comes to you. It is called *Grace* in Scripture. "Set your hope fully upon the Grace that is coming to you at the revelation of Jesus Christ." Well, *Grace* is simply an unearned, unmerited gift of God to man, and that gift is God Himself. So you are raised from the level of being a Son to the level of being the Father.

Now, let's enter the Silence.

Chapter 3

Neville (03-17-1969)

BEAR YE ONE ANOTHER'S BURDENS

The Bible is the most practical book in the world. In it we are told that one named Simon carried the cross behind Jesus. The word "Simon" means "to hear with understanding and consent to what is heard." And Jesus is your own wonderful human imagination.

The gospel tells what happens in the soul of Jesus. The events recorded there are seen and heard by none save but Him. Through these experiences He gains the certainty that He is not only the Son of God, but also God Himself. But when he tells his story few will accept it, as his experience of scripture differs greatly from its interpretation by the priests and rabbis. Simon, however, understands what he hears and, consenting to it, he carries the cross.

We are told to "Bear ye one another's burden and so fulfill the law of Christ." Now, the law of Christ is described in the Sermon on the Mount. It is a psychological law, as Christ tells you in the 5th chapter of Matthew, saying: "You heard it said of old, 'You shall not commit adultery.' But I tell you, anyone who looks lustfully upon a woman has already committed the act with her in his heart.'" (The word "heart" and "soul" are synonymous in scripture.)

When you are told in the 4th chapter of Psalms to "Commune with your own heart upon your bed," are you not communing with yourself? And in that communion are you not told that the act is committed? I tell you: the law of Christ is imaginal and you carry His burden, for "Inasmuch as we do it to one of the least of these, we do it unto Him."

Paul, seeing the meaning of Christ, said: "From now on I regard no one from the human point of view, even though I once regarded Christ from the human point of view, I regard him thus no longer." Paul realized that Christ was the pattern of salvation buried in every child born of woman, and did not seek a little Christ, but the universal Cosmic Christ buried in all.

There is only one Christ, so when you imagine, you are imagining Christ. Now, one who hears and believes this is called Simon. It is he who goes out and carries the cross by lifting the burden from the back of the one being who is carrying the entire cross; for every human is a cross, who collectively form the cross the Cosmic Christ bears.

When one hears the story and believes it, he goes out to lift the weight of every cross. Seeing someone struggle to pay rent or buy food because he is financially embarrassed, Simon lifts his cross by seeing the man gainfully employed. He does this because he knows he is doing it only to himself, as there cannot be another. As a psychological act, he represents the other to himself as he would like to see that other, and to the degree he is self-persuaded that what he imagined is true, it will become true.

Simon does not move a cross from one little point in space to another. He goes through life following Christ, as he bears the cross and lifts the weight of mankind. Many a man remains behind the 8-ball because no one ever thought he could be anything other than what he appears to be. Fortunately I had a mother who, at a tender age took me aside and persuaded me that I was her favorite. She would say: "You will make mother very proud of you, won't you?" and naturally I said: "Yes, mother." I wore long white curls at the time, and she would curl my hair, run her finger up my curl, kiss me, and send me on my way - then call the next one to have his hair curled. Mother told the same story to each of us. It was only after we had all grown to manhood that we discovered what mother had done, but by that time she had accomplished her purpose. She didn't expect us to make a fortune but to be one in whom she would be proud, and in our own separate spheres we all became successful in her eyes.

Many a man is a failure today because no one ever believed he could be otherwise. So I say to you: if you believe that there is only one being and only one cross, you will lift the cross from a seeming other, and - as Simon - follow your imagination to its fulfillment.

Every child born of woman is a cross, animated by Christ Jesus; so when you lift the burden from an infant or one of many years, you are doing it unto yourself. As you bear one another's burdens you fulfill the law of Christ; for inasmuch as you do it to one of the least of these, you have done it unto me. If you believe me and put your belief into practice, you are bearing the cross. But if you are so engrossed in your own little world that you cannot see another as a projection of yourself, you do not believe me and will not become a Simon. Only as you believe and act, will you bear the cross as Simon, enter the temple in the Spirit, and - finding the child - take him up in your arms and say: "Lord, let now thy servant depart in peace according to thy Word, for my eyes have seen the salvation of God."

Called a little child in the Book of Luke, God's creative power is symbolized as the unveiled arm in the Book of Isaiah. In this wonderful 53rd chapter of Isaiah, the prophet speaks of the unveiling of the arm of God as the salvation of the world. And when the prophecy is fulfilled it appears as though you are betrayed, but I ask you: what did Judas betray? He betrayed the messianic secret of Jesus and the place where he might be found.

A secret must first be heard before it can be told. I have betrayed the messianic secret in my book called Resurrection, so I have played the part of Judas. Having experienced the part of Jesus, I have recorded my experiences so that anyone coming after I have gone from this sphere will know the secret.

The messianic secret is unlike that which the priesthoods of the world believe. Jesus is not a little man who comes from without to save mankind. Jesus comes from within, for He is a pattern, which unfolds in and reveals the individual as the Son of God who is God. Knowing my scripture, when the visions came upon me I searched and found they dovetailed one another. I have shared my experiences with everyone who will listen; and those who hear them with understanding and accept them become Simon, who picks up the cross and eases the burden from the back of the Cosmic Christ.

When you meet someone who is unemployed and take a moment to imagine him gainfully employed, you are Simon. Practice this art daily. Pick up your cross and set everyone free from what he seems to be. That is how you bear one another's burden and so fulfill the law of Christ, which is all imaginal.

If you hear this message with understanding you will go out and fulfill the law of Christ. If you do not understand me you may not agree, but I tell you: this is the most incredible story that can ever be told. You need not have a brilliant mind to accept it. In fact, the more brilliant your mind is, the less chance this concept will be believed, yet I tell you it is true. Everyone who accepts it will one day experience scripture within himself, for the gospel is nothing more than that which happened within the soul of Jesus, who is Jehovah, who is the Lord, in you.

Jesus is your awareness of being, your I AM. It is He who hears the story and either accepts or rejects it. If you think of a man who lived two thousand years ago when I use the word "Jesus," you will not see the Jesus in everyone; for Jesus is awareness, sound asleep and carrying a tremendous burden as His dream. If you will accept my story, Jesus will begin to awaken as you lift his burden and carry the cross behind your imagination. Simon is first seized, and then the cross is placed upon him as the individual who hears and understands and consents to what he has heard.

If you really believe me you will not pass anyone without doing something to lift his burden. Taking up his cross, you will represent him to yourself as you would like to see him; and to the degree that you are self-persuaded, he will become it, even though he may never know what you did. Things will happen in his world and he will become what you conceived him to be, not knowing who did it...but who did it? Christ, for there is only Christ in the world. You can take no credit in the doing, because you are only doing it to yourself.

As you represent another to yourself as you would like to see him, you are lifting his burden and fulfilling God's law. And when your time is fulfilled you will enter the temple and find the sign of the birth of your creative power as a child wrapped in swaddling clothes. Then the arm of God, who creates everything, is unveiled in you and from that day on whatever you imagine will come to pass - I don't care what it is. I ask you to dwell upon this thought and follow the pattern of Simon. Lift the burden of someone today, and maybe tomorrow you will be able to do it to two. Don't let another remain carrying his burden, because there is no other. Lift his burden from yourself and follow Jesus Christ, your own wonderful human imagination.

The dream of life begins with the call of Abraham, and comes to its climax and fulfillment in Jesus Christ. Everyone must and will experience that climax. Then the curtain will come down and you will leave this sphere to join the heavenly brotherhood, who contemplates this world of death saying: "What seems to be, is- to those to whom it seems to be." Take that one little statement: what seems to be is to those to whom it seems to be. You can assume any state and persuade yourself that it is so, and it will become so. Torments, despair, and eternal death will also seem to be, "But Divine mercy steps beyond and redeems Man in the body of Jesus"; for in the end there is only one body, only one Lord, and you are that one Jesus Christ. You will wear that one Risen Body as your own and be the one Spirit that inhabits it. And you will know yourself to be that one Spirit who is the Lord of all.

Today you are not aware of your true identity, but Paul made it very, very clear in his 2nd letter to the Corinthians, when he said: "If we have been united with Christ in a death like his, we certainly shall be united with him in a resurrection like his." Do you see the difference in tense? We have already died with Christ, and we will live with him when God's pattern of salvation erupts and the gospel unfolds within us individually.

Now, whenever I tell my story there are always those who - knowing me by my physical origin - do not know me by reason of my spiritual birth. Seeing only the outside man called Neville, they judge from appearances and claim I am blaspheming by making these bold claims. But a few will believe me and become Simon by lifting the burden and transforming the lives of those he meets, no matter that it may seem to be.

If you want more money, better health, or the state of marriage, Simon simply hears your desire as granted, then goes his way believing that what he has heard is now a physical fact which will confront you in the near future. He never seeks your thanks, but knows your desire must come into being; for he has lifted your burden upon his shoulder and believes in his own wonderful human imagination.

When you hear and believe in God's pattern of salvation, you are believing in Jesus. Everyone contains that pattern - therefore everyone is Jesus. Leave no one distressed. Do not give from your pocket, but give them every desire of their heart from your imagination. You could give money from now until the ends of time, and not give of yourself! Only when you imagine for another are you truly giving of yourself; and as you believe in the reality of what you have imagined, are you lifting the burden you are called upon to do, thereby fulfilling the law of God.

When you feel the joy of having done it, don't wait for the phone to ring; simply go your way and lift the burden from another, and then another. An artist friend recently told me about some work he had done for a friend, but had not been paid according to their verbal agreement.

After our discussion I heard my friend tell me the debt was paid. That was all I did. Last night he told me that, seemingly out of the blue, the man came to his house and gave him a check for the full amount agreed upon. Now I will say to him that check will be multiplied over and over again, for there are many artists needing your talent to improve theirs.

Don't say something cannot be done, for the minute you do, you are placing a limit upon yourself. And don't limit your friend because of his financial, social, or intellectual background. That's a heavy cross for him to bear. Rather, lift his cross and set him free. We live in a world of horrors, but as Blake said: "Don't be intimidated by the horrors of the world. All is ordered and correct and must fulfill its destiny in order to attain perfection. Follow this pattern and you will receive from your own ego a deeper insight into the eternal beauties of reality. You will also receive an even deeper release from all that now seems so sad and terrible."

When you know this truth, you will lift the burden of all those you meet, for you will know that regardless of the pigment of his skin, the tongue in which he speaks, his belief, or nationality - you and he are one, for God is one. The great Sh'ma of the Hebrew confession of faith "Hear O Israel, the Lord our God, the Lord is one," will take on new meaning.

If God is one, there cannot be another; so in the end you and I will be the same father of the same son. I have been sent to convey that one thought to the world. I have taught it through the spoken word and recorded it in my book, Resurrection, that God's true son is David. I have now completed the work I was sent to do.

The priests do not know the mystery. They are men without vision, reading a book they do not understand. To my mother, a priest was a wise man who could not be contradicted. I never argued with my mother about that, but I knew she was wrong. As a boy I had visions and knew the priests did not know what they were talking about; but mother could not understand how her little, uneducated boy could challenge that which she considered the wise men, because they could speak Latin and read Greek. But I knew their knowledge came from study, while my wisdom came from vision.

Having matured, I have been called and sent to reveal the true Son of God who unifies humanity. We will all know that one son to be our own son, for he will reveal each one of us as God the Father. Jesus Christ in you is God the Father, and David (in you) is His son. The day will come when David will awaken in you, rise in you, and call you Father, giving you a certainty which cannot be denied. Maybe from what you have heard tonight you may change your belief, but you will never know the certainty of Fatherhood until you see David as your son. And when everyone sees David as his son, are we not the one Father?

Tonight I urge you to play the part of Simon. If you do, you will not be neglecting but helping yourself; for as told us in the story of Job, as he prayed for his friends his own captivity was lifted. While locked in his own desire to free himself of his physical, social, and financial problems, Job forgot himself and prayed for his friends, and in so doing all that he had lost returned to him one hundred fold. As you pray for your friends you will discover your own captivity is lifted; your cross becomes lighter and lighter until finally you are light itself. So take my yoke upon you and learn from me, for my yoke is easy and my burden is light. Ask for no thanks or financial gain in the doing; just know the joy of lifting the cross, for it is being lifted from your own shoulders. When I hear that a man's needs have been provided for and he has become self-persuaded, it is true and it becomes true. I never tell him what I did. I simply revel in the joy and satisfaction of seeing this law of Christ fulfill itself. It never fails when put into practice.

Believe in the reality of your own imaginal acts, for faith is loyalty to unseen reality. Have faith in your imaginal act. Although unseen by the outer world as an external fact, your loyalty to its unseen reality will cause the unseen to become seen by the world. This is the practical side of this night. You and I can lift the cross from our own shoulders; for as I lift your cross I am lifting mine, and in a way I do not know the burden is lifted from me. Everyone you meet is yourself made visible, for there is nothing but yourself in the world.

As you read these passages I have quoted tonight, pull them together and you will have a beautiful mosaic. Remember, when you do it to one of the least of these you have done it unto me, the one the world is seeking. You may see me as an insignificant little man, but I am Christ, the Lord God Jehovah. Lift my burden for even the most insignificant other, and go your way. You may not recognize your harvest, as you may not remember the favor you granted another many years ago. Seeing him healthy and financially secure today you may forget what you did, and maybe even he will have forgotten he ever asked your help - but what does it matter? The burden has been lifted. Go forward and play the part of Simon, and the day when you least expect it you will find the symbol of your creative power as a child wrapped in swaddling clothes. And then the 53rd chapter of Isaiah will be fulfilled, as your arm of God is revealed.

When scripture unfolds within you, you will know a thrill that is beyond ecstasy. Then you will no longer see scripture as secular history. You will know from experience that the story is supernatural, and has nothing to do with history as we understand it. The events spoken of by the apostles did not take place on earth, but in the soul of man as he walks the earth.

I have shared with you that which took place in my soul in the hope that I will find a few who will believe me to the point of putting my words into practice. I have unveiled myself to those who believe, and now they are beginning to be unveiled - while the rabbis and the priests who see me as an impostor remain veiled. Even to this day, when Moses is read the veil is on their minds. I pray for all of them because they are blinded to the truth by their refusal to accept any change in their fixed belief. I have come to do one thing: to make clear to the entire world who the true Son of God is who will unify the world.

Jesus Christ is God the Father and his son is David. When David calls you Father, you will know you are Jesus Christ, the Lord. If I am God the Father, who is my son? David. I tell you, David is not a physical being. It is in Spirit that he calls you Father, and scripture is fulfilled. Everyone will be called Father by the one being who is David, and if he calls you Father and he calls me Father, are we not the same being? Are we not the one God and Father of all? I tell you, without loss of your individual identity, you will know that you and I are one. Now let us go into the silence.

Frank Carter Lecture Series

Frank Carter Lecture 1: Dated 6/6/76

Frank Carter: I decided to tell this story about Neville. I decided to use my middle name which is Eammon's. It was my mother's maiden name. My authority rests on the fact that I spent Neville's last day with him. As you all know Mrs. Goddard was quite ill and she was in the hospital.

So, Neville as far as I can figure knew exactly he was going because he left two documents. One is a formal document and the other is a handwritten note. Now what had happened was that three years before he departed I had the vision of his death as Judas. At the time, I didn't know what it was, I saw Neville in front of a restaurant and I started to speak to him and suddenly he chocked and he fell back and when he fell on the sidewalk he spilled all of his bowels.

Well the dream was so grisly that I simply couldn't tell him and yet at that time he was saying from the platform, "I love to hear that you have seen me die". Well I kept hearing him say this, but I still could not bring myself to tell him this awful dream which I'd had.

So, one night I was leafing through scripture and suddenly my eye fell on this passage in the first chapter of Acts. This is the description of Judas, Peter is speaking-- Can everyone hear?

Male speaker: You can speak a little louder.

Female speaker: [inaudible 00:02:28 - 00:02:32]

Frank Carter: I was going through scripture and my eye fell on the description of the death of Judas in the first chapter of Acts. Now Peter is speaking here. He is describing Judas who was numbered among them in the ministry and he says, "Now this man with the reward of his iniquity purchased a field and falling headlong he burst asunder in the midst and all his bowels gushed out".

Well I was so excited I could hardly wait to tell Neville, but it was too late at night. So, I practically sat up all night and when I figure that it was a decent hour in the morning I got on the phone and I got Mrs. Goddard on the phone too because I wanted her to hear this and I told him. I said, "Neville you are Judas" and he said, "Yes". Judas betrayed the Messianic secrets and then he said, "You know that there are two traditions of the death of Judas". One is in the Gospel account where he goes and hangs himself. The other is this account which I just got through telling you how he bursts asunder in the midst and all of his bowels gush out.

Then he went on to say, "In the orient suicide is a very honorable thing. The one who commits suicide in the orient disembowels himself" and then he repeated once more, "Judas betrayed the Messianic secret". Now just in case there should be someone here who did not hear him toward the last I want to mention that his truly great experience was the discovery that he is the father of David and he told all of us that we are to have the same experience. We are going to awaken as God the Father.

Now what I am telling today would have no purpose it would make no sense whatsoever if it were not for the fact that every lecture Neville said, "I am not speculating, I am not theorizing, I have awakened as God the Father and every one of you is going to have this experience". So that laid the groundwork.

Then that last day we were going to a dinner party, a very early dinner party, and I literally spent the whole day with Neville and I'm positive I'm the last one who saw him here. So, I went to his home to pick him up and he was so happy because he felt that Mrs. Goddard would soon really be well and she was coming back from the hospital, but now Neville was so anxious not to disappoint his hostess that he left Mrs. Goddard in the hospital one day longer so he could go to this dinner party.

Now I know in retrospect that he left her in the hospital because he did not want her to see his body. So, on the way to the hospital I told him about a dream I'd had the night before and then I had awakened with great great anxiety and he said to me, "It's wonderful that the depths of your being have given you a warning". Now I know now that the anxiety I awoke with was my inner self telling me in advance of what was about to happen.

So, we went to the hospital and I went downtown to do a few errands and when I came back I told him about my trip downtown. I said, "It was so hot, terribly hot, but it made me think here we are deep deep in the heart of woodland" which was Blake's term for this earth, the furnaces here on this earth and he said, "Yes, we are in woodland and there are those who believe that no one ever returns from it" and I said, "Do you see those who haven't come in?" and he said, "Yes, I see them" and I said, "You see those who have come out?" and he said, "Yes, I see those" and I said, "Then you see all three" he said, "Yes, I do and those who have come out who have returned to eternity are the most exalted beings you could ever imagine".

When we arrived at the party the first thing we wanted was a martini. So, I got mine and he got his and then he gave me the first piece of bread and cheese. He said, "Here Frank, take this" so I took it and then just before we ate my hostess asked me if I would like to have another martini, I said, "Certainly" and Neville said, "Wait. Here Frank, take this" and he took his unfinished martini and poured it in to my glass. So, I finished his drink. I don't think I have to point out the parallel here between the Last Supper and what he was enacting there. Then after dinner he suddenly stood up and he said, "We're going" and with that we left.

When we got home to his place both of us decided that we didn't care for anything else to drink that night and after a brief conversation I

39

went home and retired early, but for some reason I couldn't sleep. There was a dog howling outside my window. So, the next morning the phone rang and it was his daughter, she had come to get him to go pick up Mrs. Goddard, and she said, "Frank, I think daddy went during the night. Can you come over?" I said, "Certainly, I'm on my way".

So, I rushed over and when I got there the body had already been sealed off. The authorities were there, the coroner the county officials and members of the family of the daughter's friends. The coroner kept asking me what had happened, he said, "Was Mr. Goddard a heavy drinker?" and his daughter said, "Well he used to be, but not lately" and he asked me how much he had had to drink and I told him, "Well, no more" and then I remembered that he had given me the last half of his martini. I said, "Well, he didn't even have two" and I said, "Why are you asking me all these questions?" and he said, "We don't understand all the blood" and I said, "Well I don't know what you're talking about. I haven't seen the body".

With that he said, "Come with me" and he took me in to the part of the house that was closed off and there was Neville lying on his back in a rigid position with his arms stretched out like this, nude with a napkin over his face, and the coroner said, "We don't understand all the blood. See" and with that he reached down and picked up the napkin and showed me and there was the image which I had seen in my dream all those years before.

A terrible contorted expression on his face as if he had chocked to death. Now that is what I saw in my dream, I saw him choke and then fall backward and when he fell backward his bowels gushed out. Now naturally when he died here on earth his bowels didn't gush out, his blood gushed out. The coroner said, "Apparently he shed every drop of blood in his body" and with that he put the napkin back over Neville's face and then before we left he said, "We don't understand all the blood, see" and once more he reached down and picked the napkin up so I could

40

see the face.

So, I knew in that instant in a way that I could not understand a way that I could not prove that I was actually seeing scripture which was written 2,000 years ago made history because he had already told his group that he was Judas. I think some of you may remember the lecture some years ago when he talked about the dream, which one of the members of the audience had had, about his death as Judas and at that time he explained that Judah is the great revealer because the word Judah comes from Yahd which in Hebrew is the word for hand.

I didn't know how to begin what to do where I would go from there. I certainly had no proof, there was no one I could tell. I did tell a few people. Something told me to tell the two men in the family of Neville's daughters friends who had cleaned up his blood. Something told me to tell them that I had seen him die this way some years ago so that it was on record so to speak.

The following week I was in his home and I happened to go near his armchair where he spent so much of his time and there beside his armchair was a note. The note read, "Isaiah 53 first verse who hath believed our reports" following that were the words, "This is my true experience of the last supper. Judas betrayed the Messianic secret" following that in scripture, "Amos chapter eight verse

11 Behold, the days come, saith the Lord GOD, that I will send a famine in the land, it will not be a famine of bread, nor a thirst for water, but for the hearing of the word of God" following that the scripture from Isaiah 22 22nd verse to the 25th verse, "And the key of the house of David will I lay upon his shoulder so he shall open and none shall shut and he shall shut and none shall open and I will fasten him as a nail in a sure place and he shall be for a glorious throne to his father's house" and then to paraphrase the rest describes the hanging of the burden of the vessels of the fathers house on this nail and then the nail is cut off and the burden falls.

Now this note I found on Thursday. Well, when I saw that note it was as if I had gotten the telegram from eternity because I knew that this was his way of letting me know that he knew that his death was going to fulfill scripture, but I still didn't know what to do with it.

Then some weeks later I was able to see the document which he wrote as a lead in to resurrection, which as you know is his great great statement on his experience. He describes all of his experiences from the birth to the appearance of David to the splitting of the temple and then finally the benediction of the dove. Well he had told us that he wanted to write a lead in to resurrection, something that would help prepare the reader for what was coming.

I can't quote the whole thing, I started to read it too you, but I think really, it's too long so I will tell you the gist of it. He says that what happened to him goes beyond any reasonable thing, it was all revelation. That he knew that anyone hearing this story if he were in their place he would think, "Well poor Neville he must of had a very hard time of it" then he goes on to make the assertion that Jesus is the I Am of every man in this world and his son the Christ is David. Then he says, "Until I got this down on paper I didn't feel that I had accomplished the work which I was sent to do" Then he goes on to say, "I now present my two witnesses, the internal witness of my experience and the external witness of scripture".

So, between the lines he is telling us that he knew perfectly well that he was sent in to this world by the Elohim, that is to say the brothers the compound unity, which is God. Sent here to the characters in the play to let them know the means by which they were to depart from this play.

A few days before our dinner party I called him to tell him that I was having a very very high experience. I couldn't account for it, but that my consciousness was going higher and higher and higher and I said, "Neville, I know beyond a shadow of a doubt that some kind of authority is going to be given to me. I don't understand it, I certainly

42

didn't earn it" with that he broke in and he said, "No, it's all a gift. It's all grace" and I said, "Well, that's my story" and he said, "Do you want to hear my story?" and I said, "Yes" he said, "Mrs. Murphy went off to Lourdes to see the Holy Relics and while she was there she saw the braces and she saw the crutches and when she was coming back through customs a customs inspector said, "Mrs. Murphy do you have anything to declare?" and she said, "Why no" and he said, "Well do you mind if I open your suitcase just the same?" and she said, "Why no, help yourself" So he opened the suitcase and looked around and he found a bottle and he said, "What is this Mrs. Murphy?" she said, "Why I've been to Lourdes to see the Holy Relics and I've brought back a bottle of holy water" he said, "Do you mind if I inspect it?" and she said, "No no by all means" so he opened it he sniffed at it he tasted it, he said, "Mrs. Murphy this is not a bottle of water this is a bottle of scotch" and she said, "Down on your knees and pray to the Holy Father it's another miracle"". [laughter]

So, I am sure you're not surprised that he announced his coming demise in the form of a joke. I didn't get it, I laughed at it I thought it was funny, but I didn't get it until someone said, "Don't you see the first words? Went to Lourdes to see the relics" I thought well that is right there aren't any relics at Lourdes, relics in the sense of remains you simply have the crutches and the braces and what have you. So, there can be no question of doubt that he knew exactly what was coming.

He had enough control, as I see it, that he was able to arrange his wife not finding his body because that would of been a terrible blow to her. If she had seen what I saw it would of set her back terribly. Now are there any questions?

Harry: Frank.

Frank Carter: Yes?

Harry: Do you intend to continue some of Neville's work?

Frank Carter: I feel that I must tell what I have found. What I just got through telling you was the key to the discovery in scripture that Neville's name, both Neville and God appear in the form of Hebrew and Greek words and they don't just appear they appear in the very passages that have to do with his experience. So, this is what I feel I must tell because I feel that the people who supported Neville have a right to hear this story. Is that what you mean Harry?

Harry: Yes.

Frank Carter: Yes. I am here for four Sundays. Those of you that got an announcement of course know. After that I don't know. I'm not trying to convince anyone of anything. I was in a state of shock for about a year especially when I began finding these things in scripture I simply didn't know what to do with it. Actually, I secretly hoped that it would go away, but it didn't go away. So here I am, the last place I ever thought I would be.

Female speaker: Will you be teaching Neville's work?

Frank Carter: No, I don't feel commission to teach. He said it all especially the law, that's not my-- I'm not qualified.

Female speaker: But I mean as a study group there are many people who were interested, but still would like to speak about it and talk about it like his **[inaudible 00:25:29].**

Frank Carter: Yes, well that is my purpose in holding these sessions. If there is a genuine response after these four then I intend to go on, yes. Any more questions? Well if not then thank you for coming. I'm sorry that it was held up, but I wanted to make sure that everyone got here since I lost my room but what a gain.

[applause] Thank you.

[00:26:31] [END OF AUDIO]

Frank Carter Lecture 2: Dated 6/13/76

Frank Carter: I think I will start today by telling you one of Neville's favorite stories, you know he adored children. It seems a little girl came home from Sunday school and the parents asked her what she had learned that day and she said, "Oh we learned about Mrs. Murphy" and they said, "Mrs. Murphy?" and she said, "Yes you know good Mrs. Murphy will follow me all the days of my life".

Now what is so precious to us about that is that the little child not understanding the spiritual principle personified it she turned it in to a person. Paul in the letter to Philemon did exactly the same he took his own bowels and personified them. Now before I go on let me tell you what Paul says how he identifies himself. In the second letter of Corinthians the 12th Chapter the 11th verse Paul makes this statement, "I am become a fool in glorying" now Paul spoke both Hebrew and Greek, he was bilingual undoubtedly, he was tri-lingual because he was a Roman citizen I assume he spoke Latin as well because he ended up in Rome according to Acts.

Now when Paul says I am a fool if he takes it as a pun he is saying I am a Neval, you can hear that is a play on Neville because the word for Neville for fool in Hebrew is Neval now that word Neval also means skin bag. So, you hear Paul telling you that on one level he has become a skin bag, that is to say he has taken the cross he is incarnated he has become a man. On the other level, he is telling you about your very own self because here we are we are in these garments of flesh these skin bags. Incidentally the word for fool in English comes from the Latin word foolis which means wind bag. So, what better description could you have of the human body than it is a skin and a wind bag.

As a matter of fact, we like to call certain people wind bags, I feel like one right now. Now in the letter to Philemon Paul makes four disclosures but first let me take the bowels. He says, "I beseech you for my son Onesimus whom I have begotten in my bonds. I beseech you to receive him as my very own self, that is to say mine own bowels" Paul makes this statement. In that same letter, he makes three references to the bowels. Now the letter is so short, so very short, I believe it is the shortest document in scripture. It's so short that he wouldn't possibly of mentioned the word bowels three times unless he was trying to present a mystery.

Now let me go back to what I told you last week to refresh your memories. Three years before

Neville departed I saw him die in a night vision as Judas. Now in case you don't know the story of Judas's death we're told in the first chapter of Acts the Judas was the guide to them that took Jesus and this man with the reward of his iniquity purchased a field and falling headlong he burst asunder in the midst and all his bowels gushed out. I didn't tell it to Neville for a long time because it was so grisly. Then when he said from the platform, "I'd love to hear that anyone has seen me die".

One night I found it in scripture so I told him and he said, "Yes I am Judas, Judas betrayed the Messianic secrets" now you know the Messianic secret is that David is the son of God who reveals you to yourself as God the Father. Now Judas being described as the guide to them that took Jesus therefore is the great teacher. The word guide in Greek is the same word that is used for the followers of the way guide is derived from the same word as way and you remember that the early Christians were known as the followers of the way. Also in the second century, there was a sect obviously considered heretical by the church but a Christian sect called the Cainites who venerated Judas as the chief apostle.

Now coming back to the letter of Philemon, Philemon in Greek boils down to friend especially the friend who is kissed. Now you remember that the sign Judas gave when he betrayed Jesus and don't ever forget that you are Jesus, I'm not talking about anything historical I'm talking about the being you really are. The sign Judas gave was this, whom so ever I shall kiss the same is he hold him fast. I think you're beginning to see the connection. This letter is addressed to Philemon the one who is kissed.

So, Paul is actually Judas because if Neville was Judas and Neville and Paul are the same being because of the identical experiences therefore Paul is Judas and in this letter, he is giving you the information about the mystery of the bowels. I loved the way Neville would talk about Paul, he said, "Here is this man who apparently was the founder of the Christian religion because nowhere do you find such a discussion of the principles of Christianity as you do in the letters of Paul". Now Neville said, "Even though he was supposed to have been in all the best jails in all the ancient world there is no record of him none whatsoever".

Now when you read a man's word your reading his mind, he is revealing his mind to you. Now who is Paul? Again, let's look at the Hebrew because he was thoroughly a Hebrew. The word Paul in Hebrew mean verb it not only means verb it's also the formal name for a part of the verb like we say present tense past tense and so on in English. Now another formal name for the verb in Hebrew is Niffel, I don't have to point out how close to Neville that is and if you remember that in our own English tongue V converts to P because we don't say I have to go we say I have to go, so there you have the V converting to P.

So, Paul is the word. Another meaning for Paul is maker, do you remember in the Old Testament your maker is your husband, that's God. So here we have Paul the word the verb telling you that he because a Neville a skin bag. He's telling you that he took on human form actually these words were written by you because you are the Elohim the one made up of many, the one who wrote the story and came down

47

here in the story.

Now getting back to the letter of Philemon the first point Paul makes is that he is a prisoner, "I Paul a prisoner of Jesus Christ" the next point he makes is about the bowels, now this letter is written to you. He says, "The bowels of the saints are refreshed by thee brother" then he goes on and says, "I beseech you for my son Onesimus whom I have begotten in my bonds receive him as my very own self that is mine own bowels" then he goes on the next part of the letter to make the point that he is Paul the aged. Now there is some difference of option among Greek scholars as to how this should be translated.

Some scholars think it should be aged in the sense of presbyter others think it should be translated ambassador. So, he's telling you he is the aged he is the ambassador. The last point he makes in the letter is for you to prepare a lodging for him because he will undoubtedly be sent to you. I hope that if you haven't read the letter you will read it when you get home, it's very short. So here in this letter we have Paul who is the word who has made the point elsewhere that he is Neville telling you the mystery of the bowels telling you that he is the ambassador and to reserve a place for him because he is coming.

Now allow me to share an experience I had before Neville departed. I saw him one night as the fool, he was dressed in cap and bells he was wearing a tutu he looked absolutely idiotic and he was dancing across the stage like a soft shoe dance and I hesitated to tell him because you know how dignified he was, but I told him anyway and his eyes just danced because he knew. He knew scripture so thoroughly that he knew that he was the fool.

Another experience I had in a dream I ran in to a friend of mine who is called David, so you might say that I found David and then as I was leaving him Neville suddenly appeared just like that and grabbed me by the shoulders and kissed me on the cheek and disappeared immediately. When I thought about it the next day I thought well yes it

48

all makes sense because I know that Neville is Judas and Neville kissed me, so if he kisses me I know who I am because in scripture the one who is kissed by Judas is Jesus and I hope that you don't think that I'm setting myself up as someone unusual.

So, I got up and went to my bible and practically opened to the story of Neval and David in the Old Testament. It's in the first book of Samuel the 25th chapter. The whole chapter is about Neval the fool his wife Abigail and David, it's a complete parable of the story of the meeting between Neville the fool and David who is his son. But its told in such a dramatic way that you could never understand it until the story has been fulfilled by the one it was written about because Neval in the story is painted as a heavy a bad guy.

So, anyone who was acquainted with Neville would say, "Well this couldn't be because you simply couldn't find anyone better than Neville anyone kinder anyone more loving, so how could this be the same one?" The story opens with Neval, incidentally I'm pronouncing the b as a v because in Hebrew b and v are interchangeable sounds. As a matter of fact, you're likely to hear two Hebrew speaking people arguing about whether its b or v. So, I'm saying Neval.

The story opens with Neval shearing his sheep. Now there are only three characters in scripture who shear their sheep even though this is a very very ordinary thing and having to do with the importance of the economy in the ancient world, only three characters are described as shearing their sheep. They are Laven Judah, who is Judas, and Neval. Now the interesting thing is that Laven is Neval spelled backwards. Neval is spelled Nbl Laven is spelled Lbn, it's the same name. Hebrew is read from the right to the left. So, if you were reading it in Hebrew it would be Neval, if you were reading it in English it would be the same as if you had read it backwards and right in the middle is Judah.

Now we've already established that Judah was Neville and Paul. So

49

here he is in the company of these other two supposedly who sheared their sheep. Now David is in the wilderness and he hears that Neval is shearing his sheep. David's band of men had protected Neval's men, protected them from outlaws. So, David sends word by his young men that he would like because of this service he has performed he would like for Neval to send him some provisions if possible, they need food they need drink and he ends it by saying if you can give this to your servants and to your son David. David calls Neval father when he says this.

Neval instead of responding repudiates any obligation to help David, as a matter of fact he says, "Who is David and who is the son of Jesse?" now where did he get this information? David did not send him this information and yet Neval knows that David is the son of Jesse which is the same as I am. David is the son of the being whose name is I am. David is so furious that he decides to kill Neval and all his men, he swears that he will do it, but one of the young men gets wind of this and goes to Abigail Neval's wife. Now Abigail in Hebrew means father of joy. You know that a man's wife is his emanation, that is to say that thing that flows out the personality the spirit the soul. Neval thought this very definitely.

So, in scripture when you hear of a man's wife it's not talking about sex on this level as we understand it marriage in that sense it is talking about one being and the two aspects. The man the garment and the man's wife which is the life the emanation. Abigail decides to send David provisions. Now among the food that she sends are two bottles of wine. Now the word bottle in Hebrew is Nebel, she sends two Nebels of wine. She rides as scripture says on the ass on her way to meet David. Now you know that the ass is the symbol for the body, it's not talking about the animal of the beast of burden but the human body. So here is another way of saying that the father of joy is riding on the human body. The father is incarnated in the human body.

When she gets to the place where David is she lights off the ass and falls at David's feet and she says, "Don't take your vengeance out on my husband Neval he's a fool as his name is so is he folly is with him" then she says, "Neval is his name" now at this point let me tell you that Neville had his name assigned to him, some of you may know the story that when he was just a few days old his mother was pondering what to name him and all of a sudden a voice spoke out, "His name is Neville" and she looked around there was no one. About this time his uncle walked up the stairs and she said, "Did you say anything?" and he said, "No, but the babies name is Neville" so that's how he got his name.

Now let's return to the passage in this 25th chapter of first Samuel the 25th verse. Neval is his name, the same words as the announcement which his mother heard except that its turned around. Then David after she has finished speaking says, "Blessed be the Lord God of Israel who sent you to me this day" So David in spirit sees his own father who is the wife of Neval the fool and this is the story which Neville told. I'm sure he knew that story was in scripture why he never told it I don't know perhaps he was too modest.

But here Neville the historic man who actually has this experience and its written in scripture in terms of his own name. So, you have Paul as Neville Paul as Judas Paul as the fool Neville as the fool, what I'm getting at is that the man name Paul in scripture had all of the experiences of scripture. Neville repeatedly said, "I'm not theorizing I'm not speculating I have experienced the whole book" Paul's name was changed from Sol. Now the name Sol means in Hebrew asking, that is to say asking in the sense of searching, searching for the father searching for truth.

After he finds the truth his name is changed to Paul which means maker and verb. That is to say he discovers who he really is, the being he really is. Now this is what happened to Neville. He had these

51

experiences and he awoke as God the Father then he felt he had the responsibility to tell it to us. I'm sure you remember his experience of see the large quartz and as he looked at it, it fragmented. It broke in to a million pieces and then as he looked at it contemplating it, it suddenly reassembled as his own glorified form as Buddha in the lotus posture. So, he was looking at his very own being.

Now Jacob in the Old Testament wrestled with a night visitor, wrestled all night and as the morning approached the being he was wrestling with said, "Let me go because dawn is breaking" and he said, "I won't go until you bless me" and the being said, "Very well you're no longer Jacob you are now Israel" he changed his name to Israel which means he rules as God. Now the name Jacob means supplanter, the one who is able to take the place, the one who is able to use his imagination to get whatever he wants.

Now that's what Neville taught for years the principle that imagining creates reality, that you can have anything in this world you want. So, when Jacobs name was changed to Israel he named the place where it happened Pennual which means face of god. Now that's a strange thing to name it. According to the events he wrestled all night then he prevailed his name was changed and then he names it face of god. This is explained the next morning when his brother Esau arrives. Now if you remember the story Jacob had stolen Esau's birthright and Esau hated Jacob for that reason and Jacob was very afraid to face Esau the next day.

Now you must remember that they were twins, that is to say they were lookalikes. It's really the mystery of the outer and the inner man the twins are that mystery just as a man and his wife are not man and wife on this level but the mystery of the garments and the being who is wearing the garment, they're one. So, Esau and Jacob are actually one being but its told in a story form so that it will make an impression. So listen to what Jacob says to Esau the next day. He calls him my lord and

52

he says, "I saw my lords face as it were the face of god". So here in a parable Jacob is telling you that he saw his own face as god in other words he realized that he is the being that he was seeking.

Paul in first Corinthians 13th chapter is hinting that this experience that he had the same experience which Neville had, he says, "For now we see through a glass darkly but then face to face" and that word glass means mirror and you look in a mirror for only one reason, to see that which you cannot see, otherwise your own face. So, Paul is telling you that you're going to see your own being face to face and this is exactly what Neville taught.

Now are there any questions? I hope I have made this clear, I don't thoroughly understand it myself but it's all there and I hope that you will dig it out.

Female speaker 1: Is Neville the person who wrote **[unintelligible 00:33:10]**.

Frank Carter: The same. He lectured for years on imagining creates reality and then he had this tremendous experience but when he started telling it there were only a few who could accept it. I was struck by the beginning of the story of Neval. It says this man was very great, he had 3,000 sheep and 1,000 goats and I thought that isn't unlike Neville at the time he had his experience. I'm sure he had an audience of at least 3,000 and another 1,000 so probably 4,000 people.

I wasn't going to bring this up. I don't want to push the literal too far, but he said, "Scripture is more literally true than you would dare to believe". Yes Harry.

Harry: How did you come across the story of Neval?

Frank Carter: I had the night vision of running in to my friend David and just as I was leaving David Neville suddenly appeared and grabbed me by the shoulders and kissed me on the cheek and then disappeared just like that and I got up the next morning and went straight to my bible and the book practically opened itself. Any other questions?

Well we're here for two more Sundays. Next Sunday I'm going to speak about Neville Moses and

Paul, again the identical experiences. Yes.

Harry: Can I ask another question?

Frank Carter: Alright.

Harry: You're bringing these particular explanations that you're giving here for a reason, for what particular reason? What is it you want to do from you own?

Frank Carter: I don't know. I have to get it out. My doctor said, "What happened to your blood pressure?" and I said, "What do you mean?" he said, "It's too high" and I said, "Oh for heavens sakes" and I tried to tell him a little bit of this and he said, "I'm not surprised to hear that" The complete diplomat. So, then he said-- I said, "I have all of this on my chest. I feel like I'm supposed to do something with it, I'm supposed to tell. I've told a few people but I'm frustrated".

Female speaker 1: [inaudible 00:37:03] you can't keep it in.

Frank Carter: You can't keep it in, no.

Female speaker 1: [inaudible 00:37:06]

Frank Carter: I'm very nervous telling it but I must, I have no choice.

Female speaker 1: [inaudible 00:37:14] will be there to hear it and I'm sure **[inaudible**

00:37:20] and those that do understand are grateful.

Frank Carter: Thank you. Yes?

Female speaker 2: Where did this man Neville teach and when did he **[inaudible 00:37:36]**.

Frank Carter: It was exactly three and a half years April Fool's Day. Again, the fool. He I believe was here from 1954 to the time of his departure in 1972, October the 1st 1972.

I suddenly thought of something. Mrs. Goddard whenever she spoke of his departure referred to it as his ascension. I never asked her to explain it, she never offered to, but I assumed that she had had some experience. I know that in February of 1974 she fused with him, again she did not give me the particulars she gave the information to me as a throwaway. She said, "Oh by the way when I fused with Neville" when you fused with Neville, but that's all she would tell me. So, it must have been a very grand experience.

Female speaker 2: Is there such a thing as a biography of his life or biographical account that one can get in the library or somewhere like that?

Frank Carter: No, I don't believe there is. I can' think-- Yes Ann?

Ann: Would you write such a thing Frank?

Frank Carter: I could try.

Ann: The way **[inaudible 00:39:26]** I think that maybe you have **[inaudible 00:39:30]** anyone.

Frank Carter: Your answering really the question which earlier I said I don't know the answer to, namely what am I to do with this. Well I realized that eventually I must put this down on paper, but I'm no writer and I have no way of knowing how long it would take me to organize this material and get it down on paper in an acceptable form.

That was another reason I decided to lecture although I don't feel that's my strong point. I felt that you who supported him have a right to hear these things and not to wait until I can get it down on paper.

Ann: And we want you to.

Frank Carter: Thank you. Yes.

Frank Carter: Yes, you can get them from Devorss and Company. Devorss.

Female speaker 3: [inaudible 00:40:30] **Frank Carter:** That is D-E-V-O-R-S-S. **Female speaker 3:** [inaudible 00:40:40] **Frank Carter:** Yes, it's in Marina Del Ray.

Harry: There are only two that are available right now Frank [unintelligible 00:40:51] out of print now and only his first book Faith is your Fortune and the Book of Resurrection are the only two that are available right now. [inaudible 00:41:07] used book store [inaudible 00:41:13].

Frank Carter: Or use your imagination, good one Ray. **Female speaker 3:** But resurrection [inaudible 00:41:22]. **Frank Carter:** Yes.

Female speaker 3: Like the bible you're getting [inaudible 00:41:27].

Frank Carter: Any more questions? Yes Harry?

Harry: I still have either three or four new copies of Faith is your Fortune [unintelligible 00:41:47] Faith is your Fortune, I don't have any Resurrection but I can get some if they want to hear.

Frank Carter: Well if there are no more questions then thank you for coming. Yes Harry?

[00:42:11] [END OF AUDIO]

Frank Carter Lecture 3: Dated 6/20/76

Frank Carter: Is this a loudspeaker?

Male speaker: It's going to be yes.

Frank Carter: It's going to be okay. So, I don't want to talk to-

Male speaker: If you want just talk a little bit to give me your volume we can set it.

Frank Carter: Right, well then, I would say that we're starting late because some of the people haven't come back, they stepped out and testing one two three four. How's that is that alright? Good.

I don't want to talk too soft I don't want to talk too loud.

Male speaker: The way you're like now.

Frank Carter: Now today I am going to reverse the order of the lectures. Those of you that have the printed program will notice that the lecture today would have been Neville Moses and Paul, but today I'm going to give the last lecture which is Neville Lazarus and Paul.

I feel that today is the time to introduce what is really the most startling part about Neville's message and Neville's fulfilment of scripture. Neville fulfilled the most ancient religion in the world by his arrival and his message. The first lecture I gave the question came up about the Trinity, some of you may remember that question and then a gentleman volunteered the information that he had discovered that in the bible there is no mention whatsoever of the Trinity. Well at that point I had already given my lecture and I realized that if I took that up I would be giving another whole lecture. So, I dropped it until this future time.

Now the man who formulated the doctrine of the Trinity was Augustine, he's known as Saint Augustine. He as a member of the

57

Catholic Church before that he was a Pagan. Now listen to his words, he said, "That which is known as the Christian religion existed among the ancients and never did not exist from the very beginning of the human race" I'd like to repeat that, "That which is known as the Christian religion existed among the ancients and never did not exist from the very beginning of the human race".

That religion of which he was speaking was the religion of Osiris the Egyptian religion of resurrection. It must come to mind immediately that this was Neville's great theme, resurrection. He claims to have been resurrected in the spirit by seeing his son David. The Emperor Hadrian in the second century when Christianity was just beginning to start had this to say, "Those who worship Osiris are likewise Christians even those who style themselves the bishops of Christ are likewise worshipers of Osiris".

If someone said to you have you seen the prince, either you wouldn't respond immediately or you would say which prince? The photomap prince or the royal prince? How does it sound?

Male speaker: [unintelligible 00:05:00].

Frank Carter: Thanks, unaccustomed as I am to public speaking. I thought I could hear an explosion. Thank you.

So, you would say which the photomap prince or the royal prince, in other words here we have a play on words. So, you have to establish whether a thing is being referred to or a person is being referred to. In the 57th Psalm David who was the author of this Psalm says awake my glory awake my psaltery. Now that word psaltery in Hebrew is Nebal, again the word Neval which is a play on Neville which is a form of Neville.

Last week I explained the story of the fool which is the story of Neval the fool who found David and then knew that he was the father of the eternal son. This is in the 25th chapter of first Samuel. I also explained that in the greater sense it pertains to you. I hope you won't be offended if I tell you that you are the fool. You are the one here in the

58

skin bag, that's another meaning of Neville, skin bag, that's our condition. We came down in to incarnation and we're wearing these garments of skin.

Now when he says awake my glory awake Neval or Neville, which Neville? Does he mean the fool or does he mean the musical instrument because another meaning for Neville in Hebrew is psaltery which is a musical instrument. Now as the Hebrew scholars will admit that they don't even know what this instrument is, the best they can do is hazard a guess. In psalm 92 these words occur, "I will sing praises unto the name of the most high" and then follow the words, "upon an instrument of 10 strings". Now the Hebrew words here are upon my Neval and upon my Assar, which is the Hebrew word for ten, but here an instrument of 10 strings. Now again they don't know which instrument this is.

In psalm 144 are these words, "I will sing a new song unto thee oh God on the Neval Osier" again a musical instrument comprised of these two names Neval and Assar" they don't know which instrument this is either. Now from my dreams and my experiences I maintain that this is a reference to Neville the historic messenger the one who is to arrive reveal the secret and then when he has done his work he departs as Judas and that is exactly what happened.

Now the ancient name for Osiris in Egyptian is Assar, the same word as the Hebrew word for 10. So here you have the beginning of the revelation of the mystery. The Egyptian religion of resurrection. Now the story of Osiris or Assar is this, through treachery he was compelled to lie down in a coffin, the treachery was will you try it out, will you see if you fit in it and he did. Then after when he was in this coffin they closed it and then killed him and then his body was dismembered, cut up in to 14 pieces. In other words, he was fragmented and these memories were strewn all over the land of Egypt.

Then his wife Isis regathered fragments one by one and reassembled the body and after the body was reassembled his son Horus resurrected

59

him by calling to him and when he called to him he said, "El Assar come forth" and that is when Assar El Assar rose from the dead and came forth. Now at this point it must strike you as a ridiculous myth absolutely fantastic, but you must remember that this story this religion is the religion of the mind that built the great pyramid, probably the greatest monument in the world.

Investigations have disclosed the fact that the great pyramid is built on an exact knowledge of the size of the earth. It's a replica of the northern hemisphere, the ratios are perfect. I don't have the facts well enough at hand to go in to this thoroughly, but it is a replica of the northern hemisphere showing that they knew the exact measurements of the earth and that they knew the earth was round. Now we had just emerged from 16 centuries of darkness. We're just now coming in to our scientific glory, but this far back in history the ancients demonstrated their great wisdom. So, this is the religion of that mind.

Now as I told you last week, actually this is the same story told over and over and over, the names are changed you might say. The fool is the one incarnation because the fool is wearing the body wearing the garment. Now to the ancients the great symbol of this incarnation was the mummy. I don't know about you but I'm fascinated by them. I don't know why I can't explain it, it should be a dreadful thing but for some reason it's fascinating.

As a matter of fact, leafing through a magazine one day I ran upon an Egyptian antiquity shop on La Cienega so I went over and they have a mummy there and what makes it even more fantastic is that right across the street was a construction company named Lazar. El Lazar so we're in a parable, no doubt about it, everything in this world is a parable. Now to the Egyptians the mummy was the symbol of the body because the body is the coffin of the soul. The body is the coffin of the soul. On the mummy case, they inscribe the letters KRS and then the final letter T. Now you see there are no vowels in this.

60

Scholars have determined that the correct pronunciation is charast, you can hear how close to Christ that is, how close to crust and Neville's great message was that the sign of the Christ in this world is the crust of the flesh because we have come in to this experience we've come in to this great incarnation we are the Elohim. Now Judas when he committed his acts of supposed betrayal he did three things he purchased a field sold the information for 30 pieces of silver and then he betrayed by the kiss.

Now this story of the purchase of the field is conflicting. In acts, we're told that this man purchased a field with the reward of his iniquity and then falling headlong he burst asunder in the midst and all his bowels gushed out. Now this was my dream, that's how I saw Neville. I saw Neville fall backwards, I saw all his bowels gush out, he chocked turned blue in the face, it was so grisly it was so awful I couldn't tell him. Then one night I found it in scripture and I was so excited because I saw that I had experienced a parable. A parable is more literally true in this world is more literally true in the imagination than it could ever be physically.

So, I knew that I had seen the great secret of the one who betrays the Messianic secret and what is the Messianic secret? As I see it there are two parts, one is where Jesus is hiding. Now you are Jesus, Jesus is the I am of every being in this world and that's what Neville betrayed. He told you where Jesus is hiding. Now the other part of the Messianic secret is that David is the eternal son, the son who calls you father and awakens you from this world of the real this world of the play.

Now Neville then is Judas is Osiris Assar is the fool, these are all states of consciousness which he experienced. I don't think a lecture went by that he didn't say, "I'm not theorizing I'm not speculating.

I have experienced scripture from the beginning to the end and it's all true and you are going to have the same experience".

Now **[unintelligible 00:20:03]** who is here today called me the week following my first lecture. He said, "Frank I had a dream, Sunday night

61

from Monday morning the first part of my dream the depths of my soul was rejoicing because I knew the truth. I had discovered a monumental truth a great revelation, but I couldn't bring it back. I only brought back the glorious feeling" he said, "Next I found myself standing in front of Bullocks on the sidewalk and there in front of Bullocks an information centre regarding Neville was being constructed".

He said, "I was round it hadn't been completed, what I saw was the substructure or the superstructure on which the dome would rest, but it was definitely a round information center regarding Neville in front of Bullocks". He said, "Then at this point there was great controversy about the fact that this information center was obscuring their display case. So, it was moved immediately across the street and everything seemed to be fine" He said he felt compelled to tell me this dream and of course I was thrilled to death because this followed so close from my first lecture.

And then he said, "In particular he wondered about Bullocks, why Bullocks?" and I thought and I suddenly remembered a detail which I did not include in my first lecture. When I saw Neville, he was standing in front of a restaurant, it was at that point that he choked and fell back and his bowel gushed out. Now the name of the restaurant was The Golden Bull. You see how perfect this is, the depth of his being revealed a detail about this eternal story which I had not mentioned and what makes it even better is that a bullock is a young bull and the symbol of Osiris is the bull.

You probably remember when the children of Israel were in the wilderness when they couldn't see anything in sight they lost their faith, they urged Aaron to make them the golden calf because they had left Egypt and the remembered the golden calf from Egypt which was the symbol of Osiris. Now as I see it this worship of the golden calf is the worship anything external. We were taught by

Neville our guide not to look to anything on the outside but to know that your own wonderful human imagination is the only reality there is and yet there will always be those in the world who want to worship something on the outside, the golden calf, the symbol of Osiris.

So even the greatest religion in the world can be worshiped in the wrong way. No when Judas went to the chief priests he said, "What will you give me if I deliver him in to your hands?" and they said, "30 pieces of silver" they gave him the 30 pieces of silver and he went his way. Then after the betrayal and the trial Judas has a change of heart and he goes back and he says, "I have done a terrible thing, take back to silver" and they say, "We can't do it, it's the price of blood" so then Judas takes the 30 pieces of silver and throws them in to the house of the lord.

Now Judas was the treasurer because we're told he had the bag so you could call him the treasurer. In the book of Nehemiah when the children of Israel are returning from Babylon where they have been in captivity Ezra is the leader. Now the name Ezra is derived from the Hebrew word Ozar, now you can hear how close that is to Assar. The point of all this is that the Hebrew language was chosen to conceal this ancient myth and religion from the time in which it would be revealed again.

The Hebrew language abounds in the word plays on Assar. The land of Egypt itself is named after this word the present Arabic name for Egypt is [unintelligible 00:27:53] which is derived from an Arcadian word Asaru which means to delimit to delineate and ultimately to form a design to make a picture a model. Egypt itself Misryam means upper and lower limits. So, you can see from what I told you earlier about their religion this again is referring to the body. These ancients understood the mystery that we had come in to the body in to incarnation. So, this is the basis for Ezra Ozar which is a play on Assar.

In this book of Nehemiah is the discussion of placing treasure in to the treasury. Now the word for treasure is utsar, again you can hear how close this is in the 8th chapter of Nehemiah Ezra or Ozar reads out of the book to the people, they are all assembled before the water gate and when

63

he reads to the people out of the book he gives the understanding to the word so that they understand perfectly what had been written in the book. Now this is exactly what we experienced with Neville. Neville who was the messenger came to us he fulfilled the experience of Assar Ozar he read to us out of the book so that we were given understanding of what was sealed within it and then when he had completed his message he departed.

When Judas threw the money back in to the table the chief priests retrieved it and with it they bought a field which was called repotteries field. Now this conflicts with the account in Acts. In Acts, we are told that this man with the reward of his iniquity purchased a field. So here are two conflicting accounts. Another conflicting element is the fact that in the gospel account we're told that what Judas did and purchased the field by the priests was the fulfilment of what was spoken of by Jeramiah the prophet.

So, if you jump to Jeramiah you find the story in the 32nd chapter Jeramiah was instructed by the Lord to buy the field which belongs to his cousin Hanamel and so he goes to Hanamel and he offers to buy the field. Now the price of the field is 17 shekels of silver. We're told in the gospel account the price was 30 and yet we're told that this is the fulfillment of what happened. Now either you're going to dismiss this as an inaccuracy a discrepancy or you're going to look at this glaring error for a clue because remember we are in Gods mystery this Gods who done it and in the best tradition suspicion is cast on someone and then comes the working out and they're cleared and someone completely unsuspected turns out to be the culprit.

Now when you look closer at the story as its present in the gospel that you find that mixed in with that account is another account from Zachariah the chapter escapes me right now. In Zachariah, the prophet Zachariah goes to his people and he says, "give me what you think I'm worth" and they weigh him out 30 pieces of silver. Then Zachariah is told by the lord take the instruments of a foolish shepherd and at this point he breaks his staff called Banes B-A-N-E-S and departs. So, you can see that these two accounts also he is instructed to cast them in to the potter's house. Now you know that the potter is the lord, so he's instructed to cast them in to the potter's house. Now this is what Judas did he cast the 30 pieces of silver in to the potter's house.

So, I think that you are beginning to see that in the gospel account these two stories are merged in such a glaringly inaccurate way that you are forced to look for a clue.

Now going back to Jeramiah, the price is 17. Now the word for 17 in Hebrew is Sheh'-bah Assar, Sheh'-bah the word for seven means to complete, Assar which is the same word as the Egyptian god of the dead Assar is the word for 10. So, you have completed Assar. Now you remember the story of Assar was that his fragmented body was strewn all over the land of Egypt and then it was regathered and then it was resurrected by his son Horus. One of the attributes of Horus is the eternal youth. David is personified as the eternal youth. So, I think you can begin to see how close all of this is except it was concealed for 16 centuries because the ability to read the Egyptian hieroglyphics was lost.

It was only in the early 19th century when the Rosetta Stone was discovered that the ability to read ancient Egyptian was recovered. Therefore, the name Assar as the true name of Osiris was lost for 16 centuries. Getting back to the departure from Babylon and Ezra the ancient name for Assyria was Assur, then you can think about the name Asia, we pronounce it Asia but other languages pronounce it Assi Assia. Many of the ancient people the ancient religious systems have the tradition that when the gods, the incarnating legions of angels of gods were instructed to come down their name was the Asura, the Icelandic name for god is áss. In Scandinavia in their ancient religious system the pantheon of the gods was called the Assar.

So, you can see how universal this name was. Scripture itself tells us

65

that immediately after the flood there was one language in the whole earth. Noah was the survivor of the flood and through him civilization was begun all over again. I really shouldn't say this from a public platform but my personal belief is that Noah came from Atlantis, I'm not teaching this as a fact but that is my belief, but our culture the ability the scientific knowledge which built the great period and it must be over 4,000 5,000 years old, this ability must have come from a very very advanced civilization and with it came the religion.

So, wrapping this up I'm trying to show that here is a parable which we wrote before we came down, a mystery to be solved a mystery to be experienced for the purpose of awakening and we appointed one character in particular and concealed him in scripture then he came in to the world. I told you last week when his mother was wondering what to name him a voice spoke out, "His name is Neville" and then his uncle came up the stairs and she said, "Did you say anything?" and he said, "No but the babies name is Neville" and in the story of Neval the fool Abigail says those very words, "Neval is his name".

So, this man stepped out of the pages of scripture and came to us and gave us the great secret and told us that whatever we do don't worship him, don't make him in to a demigod. This is all for awakening.

Now are there any questions? Well if there are no questions that is all I have to say.

[applause]

[00:42:45] [END OF AUDIO]

Frank Carter Lecture 4: Dated 6/27/76

Frank: How's this?

Male Speaker: I think it's a little better.

Frank: Testing 1234. It's probably just about right, isn't it? Are any syllables popping?

Male Speaker: No.

Frank: Yes, it occurred to me that perhaps the lecture last week, some of you might want to ask a question.

Male Speaker: I'm sorry. If you wouldn't mind starting again.

[Laughter]

Frank: Okay, how's this?

Male Speaker: Right, ready. Just test once more and then we'll have it.

Frank: Testing, 1234. Is that good?

Male Speaker: Great.

Frank: Now I can't hear it, which doesn't mean anything, does it?

Male Speaker: Can you hear it now?

Frank: Yes. Is it just about right? Okay. During the week, I thought because of the material I introduced last week, that some of you might like to ask a question before I begin because what I presented was so unusual and so different, I thought perhaps in the intervening time, thinking about it, you might just want to ask a question before I begin. Very well.

Male Speaker: What did you say Frank?

[Laughter]

Frank: Right, that's a very good question. Right, again last week, by telling you that St. Augustine who founded the doctrine of the trinity through the Roman Catholic Church, had this to say. "That **File name: FC T2S262776.mp32**

which is known as the Christian religion, existed among the ancients and never did not exist, from the very beginning of the human race." Now that religion is the religion of Osiris, the religion of resurrection. Osiris had the name Asar, which is from the Kalian word which means to limit, to delineate a drawn plan and the very name of Egypt itself is derived from this name.

As a matter of fact, you might say that this is the religion of the mind that built the great Pyramids. The name of the country of Syria is from this name, the ancient name is Asoor. So you can see the parallel there between Asoor and Asar. Now in Hebrew this name is found in pun form, for instance the word for 10 is Asar, the word for bound or bind is Asar. The word for treasure is Unsar, the word for Maker is Asaar. Now you know that New Englanders have the pattern of dropping their final Rs, so that should present our trouble because there is no R. Another word for Maker Yansaar. I could go on and on but I think you've got the point.

Now Neville has the fulfillment of this great religion because in Scripture we find a form of Neville connected with this ancient name, except it's a musical instrument. Now I explained previously that the name Neville is from the Hebrew word Naval, which really means skin bag. Another meaning of Naval is fool, so you have the fool who is the one in the skin bag. In Psalm 144 you find these words, "Oh God, I will sing a new song to You on the Naval Asaar. Now in your King James Version it reads, "Oh God, I will sing a new song to You on the instrument of 10 strings." Now the scholars admit they don't know what this musical instrument is.

68

As a matter of fact there's a growing controversy.

A friend of mine was out here for a music convention last year, I hadn't seen him in 25 years. Somehow I got on the subject of Neville and I started telling him about the fool and I said, "Fool is Neville," and he said, "No, Neville is a musical instrument." He knew right off, he said that this has been one of his interests, tracking down the ancient Hebrew musical instruments. Now this week it came to me that the last day I was with Neville, on the way to a party. He gave a message in an offhand way, which I considered to be his last revelation about his doctrine. Somehow words were put into my mouth to say this- I had just returned from downtown where it is about as hot as it is today. And I was so impressed with the oppression of the earth experience itself. Here was the heat beating down, here were all the masses running around the downtown streets.

And I said, "Neville, I just got back from downtown and oh how deeply are in the heart of woodland." Now woodland is Blake's name for the furnaces for this earth, for the earth experience; as you say, being in the body. Then Neville took a deep breath and let out a sigh and he said, "Yes and there are those who believe that no one ever returns," and I said, "Do you see them, the brothers who haven't come in?" And he said, "Yes, I see them," and I said, "Well naturally you see those who are here because you're here and he said, "Yes, of course." And I said, "Do you see those who have returned?" He said, "Yes and they are the most exalted beings you can ever imagine." Now I said, "Well then you see all three," and he said, "Yes." I use the term 'brothers' and he used the term 'those'. He said, "There are those who believe that no one ever returns."

Now the word for God in Hebrew is Elohim, which is a plural word. Any time in the Old Testament when you see the word GOD, that word in Hebrew is Elohim and it is a plural word. Now this was Neville's last message, he was telling me, through me, that God at this point is in three divisions, all the Elohim. The Elohim who have not come in, the Elohim

69

who are here, that is we because one is all and all is one. Then the Elohim who have returned, who have received the inheritance. This of course was Neville's great theme, the promise and the promise was that you will inherit God the Father. In other words you will awaken as God the Father. Now what I want to make clear today is that you are the Elohim, the One made up of ones, the 'those'- this is all a word game; now your ancient name, the name which was lost for about 16 centuries, is Nassar because Nassar is the dead one in the underworld.

Paul knew who Asar was because when he said, "I Paul, a prisoner of the Lord Jesus Christ," in Hebrew the word for bind is Asar. Now he knew the ancient mystery of the mummy, which I think was a perfectly graphic way to present this mystery because it makes such an impression on the mind. Now the mummy was the symbol of the body, the body being the coffin of the soul. Neville often used the illustration of the beginning of Genesis and the end. It begins, "In the beginning was God," and it ends, "In a coffin in Egypt." Now as I told you last week, on the mummy case were inscribed the letters KRS, which is the word karas which means skin. And there is a modern day African word, karst, which means skin. Now to this KRS was added the suffix T, so you have the word karst and you can hear how close to Christ that is. This is where the mystery of the Christ came from, from ancient Egypt.

So that word means fleshed, in other words a God made flesh. The word Neville as I pointed out, means skin bag. Paul tells us that he became flesh when he says, "I have become a fool." The word Paul in Hebrew is another word for Maker and you recall the word for maker is Asar. Now we also have the word Paul, this word also means verb, so the verb is telling you that he came down and became flesh, became Neville. You see, it sounds like I'm talking about Neville but I'm really talking about the pattern there because his name, his ministry and his departure are all recorded in Scripture.

Not to set him apart from anyone else, I don't think he ever missed a

70

lecture but he did say, "Don't put me on a pedestal. It's all about you, the Elohim." Now last week I ended the lecture by pointing out how widespread the word Asar was in the ancient world. The very continent of Asia itself is a form of that word. Asi, we say Asia but in Greek it's Asiya. And the Scandinavian mythology, the Pantheon who were a race of gods who's called the Asar, this you can find in any modern age dictionary. Now the leader of that race of gods was named Odin, Odin was the leader of the Asar and the word Asaar is plural. He was a leader of gods. **[Unintelligible 00:16:48]** a parable, this past week I got around to reading my New Yorker magazine, at this point last Sunday I hadn't read it but I opened it up and here was a story, a very short story by Jorge Luis Borges who is one of Neville's favorite authors.

I can recall that he told several of this man's stories from the platform because they were all parables. It's as if this man was never a mystery. Now the name of this story was *The Disk*. I'm going to tell it very briefly, it's the tale of a woodcutter who lives in the words and he's never left the woods and one night he receives a visitor, an old man. He gives him lodging and food and the next day as the man is leaving, he drops his staff; the visitor does. At that point he changes completely and commands his host to pick up the staff and the woodcutter says, "Why should I?" And the visitors says, "Because I am King." So the woodcutter picks up his staff. Now the visitor goes on and says, "I am the king of the sections and I am the king of the race of Odin." At that the woodcutter says, "I don't worship Odin, I worship Christ."

The visitor goes on as if he hadn't even heard him and he says, "I am a king. Even though I lost my kingdom and I'm in exile, I am wondering this earth as a king because I have the disc of Odin." And the woodcutter says, "I don't know what that is," and the visitor opens his palm. He opens his hand
and shows his palm and he said, "Here it is. This is the disc of Odin. Of all the things in the world, it has only one side, there is nothing else in the world that has only one side." So then the woodcutter tries to get him to

71

sell the disc and the visitor refuses. At that he says, "Great greed possessed me and I was determined that I must have the disc." So when the visitor turns his back, he does him in and as he strikes the blow with his ax, the man opens his hand. And he sees when the hand opens and the palm is exposed, a glitter. Then he disposes of the body and he goes back to where he has marked the spot of the glitter and he can't find anything. Then he ends the story by saying, "I have been searching two years and I haven't found it yet."

Now I'm not going to attempt to explain this parable to you but the thing that interests me, is that here, this confrontation between Odin who is the king of the Asar and the man who worships Christ, right after I told this from the platform. So you see what a parable we're in. Now Moses knew this story well, now you know of course Moses is a state, Moses never existed as such as history. The point of the first five books of the Bible, supposedly authored by Moses, is that this mind came out of Egypt. We're told that he was raised in the house of Pharaoh, so he spoke Egyptian, he received the best education of the day. There is a legend that Moses was a priest of Osiris, of Asar. Now whether Moses was actually a priest or not is beside the point, having lived in the king's house, in Pharaoh's palace, he knew all this religion, he knew the secret of it. He knew that the mummy was simply a symbol of the body as the coffin of the soul and that Asar is the resurrected man. The one who rises from the dead.

Now in the book of John, there's a mutilation for a purpose because nothing is haphazard, it's scriptured. With the mutilation of the ancient, ancient text of the book of the dead, explaining the resurrection of Asar. He was resurrected by his son Horus who called to him as he lay in the tomb in the cave at Bethany. He went to the cave just as the central character in the book of John, when he raises Lazarus from the dead, goes to the mouth of the cave and says, "Lazarus come forth." Now in the ritual in the book of the dead, Horas says, "Al Asar come forth, Al being a title Lord, "Asar come forth." Then the dead one rises from the grave

72

and comes forth in grave clothes, which of course was the symbol of the body, the resurrection takes place while you're here in the body. It's just what Neville taught.

Now this took place in Anu in Egypt. When it was transcribed to the New Testament version, the word Beth was added, the word Beth in Hebrew means house. So you have Bethanu and in the course of time, the U converted to Y and hence you have the name Bethany. Now this existed thousands of years before the supposed event took place, which is recorded in Scripture. About a year after Neville departed, I was winding my clock one night, I have this marvelous antique clock which my mother gave to me and it was 10 o'clock and I was winding it I thought carefully and the spring gave way. So it's permanently stopped on 10, which you remember is Asar Hebrew. That night Neville was lecturing in my dream and he said in the course of his lecture, "Bethany. Now you must jump, you must skip," and, "10 and Bethany and now you must jump, 10," this went over and over.

But when I woke in the morning I thought, "Bethany, 10, Bethany, 10" so I went to my concordance and I discovered that Bethany means house of dates but there's only one problem, the word date does not occur in Scripture. So I **[unintelligible 00:27:36]** and I looked up 10 but that didn't yield anything because at that point I haven't heard of was Asar. Shortly after that someone by accident placed the right books in my hands and that was when I learned the ancient history of Osiris and the word ten. Now Moses knew the story well, you'll recall that the great revelation to Moses in the name of God was, "I am". It reads, "I am that I am." In Hebrew this reads as thus "Ehyeh asher ehyeh." You can hear how close asher is to Asar, ashur or shar. Now being bilingual, he would have to have recognized immediately that this was wordplay on that heathen god, if indeed he was a heathen god.

Now in Hebrew, the ancient Hebrew, they were no vowels, it's much like the game I'm sure you've all played in the car with the license plate and try to make words out of consonants. You don't have many vowels and you think, "I wonder what word that would spell if I use an E or an I or an O or a U?" So that was the case in ancient Hebrew, so there is no reason why that word must be translated as the word 'that', which is asher. It could have just as easily have been ashur or Asar because the letter S in this particular word looks like a three-pronged point, a trident and depending on whether a dot is placed on the right or the left, this letter for S is pronounced **[unintelligible 00:30:32]** or simply S. So in any event, this could definitely be considered a wordplay on Asar. And this was the announcement which Elohim made to Moses. Now remember you **[unintelligible 00:30:49],** you're the ones who wrote this story. So when the Elohim revealed the name to Moses, it was revealed as Asar, the ancient religion of resurrection.

Now concerning Moses, Paul said this, "I wouldn't have you ignorant and the fact that your fathers were under the cloud and that they passed through the sea and that they were baptized unto Moses in the cloud and in the sea." Now the word for cloud in Greek is nepheles, which is another form of Neville, nepheles. You see, there is no V in the Greek language and you can see that in our own English, the letter V converts to F. We say, "I 'haff' to go," we don't say, "I 'havv' to go." So these little internal changes take place. The Old Testament was translated into Greek about 250 BC, so often Paul was quoting from this Greek version which was known as the Septuagint. So here again, Paul knows Neville, he knows Neville because he is talking about the fact that the children of Israel were under the cloud and you may recall that the cloud guided them. It led the way just as Neville led the way for us.

Paul goes on and says, "They were fed with the same spiritual food." Now you know that spiritual food was the manna and if it's spiritual food, it's the Word. Neville's constant theme was the Word of God, think on the Word of God, feeding on the Word of God. Now manna actually means, "What is it?" It's from the Hebrew word mah, which means "what?" So when they found the manna the first time, they said, "Mah mah," and then

74

it was named mann, which is almost exactly like our word man. The manna was described as being like a coriander seed, white. Now the word for coriander is gad and it comes from the word godhad, which is exactly the way the English pronounce Neville's last name, which is Goddard but they say, "God-dard, Neville God-dard." Now the word for white is lavan, now lavan backwards or read in our manner from left to right, is naval. So here in this short description from the manna, that it is like coriander seed and white, you have a cryptogram Neville's name.

Also, Moses's father-in-law told him, "Be now for the people to Godward," now this is a play on words which probably only occurs in the English language. The point of the story is unfolding in the English language because that was the tongue which Neville spoke. Paul makes this statement, "We have such trust through Christ to Godward," in first Thessalonians, this statement was made, "Your faith is spread abroad to Godward." Then the author of this letter goes on to tell them that because of their faith and their understanding, because their faith is spread abroad to Godward, that they have turned aside from idols and are now worshiping the true and living God. You see, it's all a word game.

When this experience first happened, I saw all Neville's body, for some reason I told my mother this story. Now she is as orthodox as they come and I told her as much as I could in the intervening time and then came a point when I thought I should start sharing this story with those of you who supported Neville. So I went to visit her and she had sat outside the whole afternoon in her little greenhouse where we were going to talk and she said, "Son, is it going to scare me?" And I said, "I don't know but I'll tell you and it's a word game," and she sounded so relieved, "Oh good, I love games."

Male Speaker: [Inaudible 00:38:28].

Frank: Now the whole story of Judas and his death is about the death of the one reveals the great secret. In the letter of Jude, which is the same as Judas and Judan, we have a letter from the one who died and who will reveal the secret. And in it, he says that he wants to make sure that we strive earnestly for the faith which was delivered once and then it goes on to say, "Let even Michael the Archangel, when he was contending with the devil about the body of Moses, darest not deliver a reeling accusation against him but said, "The Lord rebuke you." Now what is this about the devil contending about the body of Moses? Before I go on with this, in two psalms, Psalm 16 and Psalm 108, this statement is made, "Judah is my law giver." This occurs in both Psalms. Also in the blessing of the sons of Jacob, Jacob makes this statement of Judah that the scepter shall not depart from him nor a lawgiver come out." So here again, three big statements that Judah is the lawgiver.

Now you can see that the states of Judah, Judas and Moses are being equated because Moses is very obviously the lawgiver. So then we have the great mystery of the body of Moses. He was not permitted to go over into the Promised Land but the Lord himself buried him. Now the highest level of course is this law about reveal because you are the body of God you are Elohim here incarnation and Moses is a patterned man within you who draws himself out when he is born but still we have a mystery about the body. Where is the body? Now the big mystery, historically the revelation about Neville's death is fulfilled scripture exactly. He died exactly as Judas and he left a note which was a parable but very definitely a note, explaining that he knew that he was going to die as Judas.

In Hebrews in the ninth chapter, after having discussed the new covenant in which the law is no longer written on stone tablets, that is to say on the outside; that the law was written in the hearts so no one is taught about God by anyone else. It's a great interior experience, so after [unintelligible 00:43:05] this, this news Testament, he makes this statement, "Now [inaudible 00:43:16] is a testament, a will. The terath of the one who gave it must be established because as long as a man is living, his will is not in effect. It's only after he has died and you must find the body because if there is no body, there is no will, there is no proof of demise." So on a higher plane, we think and we realize that you

76

Elohim, are the body of God and that you are already him, your own coffins are about to rise from the dead. You have received the New Testament, and this was Neville's message.

And my message is that if all the things in this world, there aren't many better documented than [inaudible 00:44:35] that when God entered this world, conducted re-administering claimed to have written scripture from beginning to end, knew that his death would fulfill scripture as Judas. So just sending out the real revelation that the most ancient religion in the world has finally been fulfilled. His ministry of revelation of resurrection, as I see it, the proof of it that it's true, that God's word is true, is [inaudible 00:45:46] of the man who made revelation, who revealed it to us. His credentials are sealed in Scripture itself, his name, and he undoubtedly knew this. Why he never told it through the platform I don't know but we don't doubt because there was a time when Neville spoke Hebrew, he was busy studying with his teacher Rehab.

It opened [inaudible 00:46:25] to him, just as it had always been there and he became so good. But he was teaching [inaudible 00:46:33] Hebrew and some of them were very outraged about this Anglo Saxon who was teaching them Hebrew. [Inaudible 00:46:49] perhaps if he knew who he was, he would be [inaudible 00:46:57] and when he arrived, and I told him that he was late and he said, "Well, where have you been? I've been waiting for you." He asked me later how I knew and I said, "The brother was telling me you were coming." Now are there any questions?

[00:47:36] [END OF AUDIO]

Frank Carter Lecture 5: Dated 10/31/76

Frank Carter: Neville came into the world, you might say he came off of the page into the world and delivered a message. This message is all about you. The important thing about Neville's giving the message is if he had not given the message you wouldn't know it. So, he revealed a truth to you, a truth that was written thousands of years ago.

On the way over here today I heard on the radio that this is the 50th anniversary of the death of Harry Houdini, probably the greatest magician in modern times. I thought that was really interesting, because today I'm going to talk to you about Neville the magician. You know today is Halloween. This is the day when people put on masks, they put on costumes, they engage in all kinds of revelry, all kinds of buffoonery. They go out and make fools of themselves, otherwise Halloween hasn't succeeded if you don't make a fool of yourself. Neville, before he had the promise, taught an audience of thousands about imagining creates reality. To someone who did not know that principle, the application of that principle and its results would truly appear to be magic, because what is magic? It's the ability to create in your world exactly what you want. I hope to show today that Neville, this magician who was also Judas, who died as Judas, is the fulfillment of the most ancient religion in the world.

This is what happened, a few years before Neville departed he told from the platform that he loved to hear that anyone had seen him die. About that time, I saw him die in a dream. The dream was so awful, as the kids would say it was so kinky, so terrible, I couldn't tell him. Yet he kept saying from the platform, "I love to hear that you have seen me die". One night when I was reading scripture I came upon the account of the death of Judas in the first chapter of Acts. Peter is talking, he's describing Judas and he says, "Judas was numbered among us. This man with the reward of his inequity purchased a field and falling headlong he burst asunder in the midst and all his bowels gushed out". Now, this is what I saw in my dream all those years before. I was riding in a car and I approached a particular restaurant. As I got closer, I saw that Neville was standing in front of this restaurant dressed as a magician. Besides that, he looked exactly like the Joker. You Batman fans know who the Joker is. His face was ashen white, a really grotesque sight. I was about to greet him, I was going to say, "Neville, what are you doing here?" At that point in front of that restaurant, Neville choked. When he choked, he turned blue in the face, and with that he fell back. When he fell back on the sidewalk all of his bowels gushed out. There he was lying on the sidewalk with his bowels fallen out.

That was the dream I didn't want to tell him. When I found it in scripture, I realized that I had seen the eternal vision which was recorded in scripture, but it's told in the form of a parable. It's told in a dramatic way. It's concealed, because Judas was painted as a heavy, as the bad guy. So for 2000 years we believed that Judas was the bad guy. When I found it in scripture, it was too late at night, I couldn't call. I was so excited I was up practically all night. When I felt that it was a decent hour the next morning, I got on the phone and I called him. I got his wife, Bill, on the phone too, on the extension. I wanted her to hear this. I told him the dream and I said, "You're Judas", and he said, "Yes. Judas betrayed the Messianic secrets". He went on to say, "God entered this world by committing suicide". Then he pointed out to me that there are two traditions in scripture of the death of Judas. The one is by hanging, and this is in the Gospel account. Judas goes and hangs himself after he betrays Jesus. The other tradition is the one recorded in the first chapter of Acts, Judas falls headlong, bursts asunder, and all his bowels gush out. Neville went on to say, "In the Orient, the honorable suicide is to disembowel oneself". You see how vivid, how graphic all of these images are. You couldn't possibly forget them, it's told in language that will make an indelible impression on the memory. Before Neville hung up he said once more, "Judas betrayed the Messianic secrets". Now it never occurred to me that there would be anything else. I was thrilled to death that I had this vision and that Neville had confirmed it.

I wasn't prepared for the fact that it would become more literally true for the imagination than any physical thing in this world could be, and yet it actually came to pass, because I spent his last day with him. Mrs. Goddard was very ill at that time, she was in the hospital. Neville was going to a dinner party, and I was going to drive him. Because he didn't want to disappoint his hostess, he left Mrs. Goddard in the hospital one more day. A few days before the dinner party I called to tell him of an experience I was having. I said, "My consciousness is going higher and higher. I feel absolutely that some kind of authority, which I don't deserve, which I didn't earn, is going to be given to me". With that he broke in and he said, "No, you don't earn it, it's all a gift. You don't earn anything in this world", but he confirmed what I said, so there can be no question that he knew what was coming.

I said, "Well, that's my story", and he said, "Do you want to hear my story?" I said, "Yes". He said, "Mrs. Murphy went off to Lourdes to see the holy relics, the crutches and the braces. While she was there she looked around and saw everything about Lourdes. On her way back going through customs, the customs inspector asked her if she had anything to declare. She said, 'No, I've been to Lourdes to see the holy relics'. He said, 'Do you mind if I look just the same?' She said, 'No'. So, he opened her suitcase and looked around and found a bottle. He said, 'Mrs. Murphy, what's this bottle?' She said, 'It's a bottle of holy water. I've been to Lourdes to see the holy relics'. He said, 'Do you mind if I inspect it?', and she said, 'No, man, help yourself'. So he opened it, he sniffed at it, he tasted it and then he said, 'Mrs. Murphy, this is not a bottle of holy water, this is a bottle of scotch'. She said, 'Down on your knees, man, and pray to the holy father, it's another miracle'". So that is the way he announced his coming death, by telling a joke. I didn't get it.

81

The day of the party I picked him up at the house, I took him to the hospital. I left him there and I went downtown to do a few errands. It was a terribly hot day. The heat was oppressive, and it was as if in my imagination I had a vision. As I looked at all of the people running around on that hot downtown series of streets, I said to myself, "Here we are deep in the heart of woodland". Woodland is Blake's word for this world, this world of the wheel, this world of the play. I went back and I picked him up at the hospital and I excused myself for a minute, and I came back a different way. I came up behind him this time and there he sat sort of hunkered over, bone tired. I tapped him on the shoulder and he looked around and he brightened up, he regained himself. I said "You weren't expecting me this way, were you?" He shook his head, and I said, "I have ways ye know not of", and he laughed, his eyes just twinkled. That was a great joke to him. I loved the look in his eyes when I said that. Those words were somehow put in my mouth, I don't know why I said it.

On the way to the party, I told him about my experience downtown and feeling that we were deep in the heart of woodland. He took a breath and let out a deep sigh and he said, "Yes, and there are those who believe that no one ever returns from woodland". I said, "You mean brothers who haven't come in?", and he said, "Yes". I said, "You mean that you see the brothers who have not come into this story?" He said "Yes, I see them". I said, "Do you see the ones who have come out?" and he said, "Yes, and they are the most exalted beings that you could ever imagine". I said, "Well then you see all three", and he said, "Yes, see all three".

When we got to the party, we got our drinks right away. All the guests had not arrived. There were some hors d'oeuvres set out. Neville went straight to them after we got our drinks, cut off a piece of cheese put it on a cracker and gave it to me and said, "Here, Frank, take this" Just before dinner, our hostess asked us if we would like to have another drink. I said, "Yes", and he declined. He took his drink, which he hadn't

82

finished and he said, "Here, Frank, take this", and he took his drink and poured it into my glass. So, I made myself another drink with what he had given me from his drink. Now I don't have to point out the parallel here between what he did and the last supper, because this was literally his last supper here on Earth.

I must go back to a few days before. I called to finalize the arrangements for the dinner party. He said, "You know, I was sitting here in the silence gathering my thoughts, and I suddenly realized something. I went in to my sweetheart and I said, 'Darling, you know the story of the last supper and Judas' betrayal? It isn't that at all. The story of the last supper is my experience of preaching the word of God. That's what it's all about.'" At that, I broke in and I said, "Yes, and don't forget that I saw you die as Judas".

After dinner at this last dinner party he suddenly stood up and he said, "We're going. I'm taking you home, Frank". So, we left. When we got to his place I stayed just a short time. Neither one of us had anything else to drink that night. I went home, I retired early. The next morning I got a call from his daughter and she said, "Frank, I think Daddy went during the night. Can you come over?" I said, "Certainly", and I went right over. When I got there, the authorities were already there and there were friends of the daughter there, friends of the family. The body was sealed off.

The coroner questioned me, "Was Mr. Goddard a heavy drinker?" With that, his daughter broke in and she said, "He used to be years ago, but not in recent years". The coroner asked me again, "Did he have a lot to drink last night?" I said, "No", and then I suddenly remembered everything that had happened about the drinks, the fact that he didn't even finish his second drink. I said, "He didn't even finish his second drink, he gave it to me. Why are you asking all these questions?" The coroner said, "We don't understand all the blood". I said, "I don't know what you're talking about, I haven't seen the body". With that he said, "Come with me". He took me into the part of the house which was sealed off, and there was Neville nude, lying on his back.

He had fallen out from his bedroom doorway on his back into the hallway, and his arms were stretched out like this. There was a napkin over his face, and the coroner said, "We don't understand all the blood, see?" With that he reached down and pulled up the napkin off of his face, and there was the face I had seen in my vision, that choked, agonized expression, and there was blood all over his face. The coroner said, "Apparently he shed every drop of blood in his body". Now you'll recall that Neville forecast that when he went it would undoubtedly be another massive explosion, because his other experiences had begun with an explosion. The coroner put the napkin back on his face and as we were about to leave once more he reached down and picked up the napkin and showed me the face again and said, "We don't understand all the blood". I was in a state of shock. It was as if a million facts had gone through my mind like a computer, because I realized that I was seeing the word made history. I was not prepared for such a literal enactment.

The following week I was in the home. Mrs. Goddard had returned from the hospital, and I went close to his big, black leather armchair, the place where he spent so much of his time. There prominently displayed beside the armchair on the table was a note. There were three scripture quotations and one short sentence, "This is my true experience of the last supper. Judas betrayed the Messianic secret". Just a few days before his departure he had completed a lead in to *Resurrection*, his book, *Resurrection*, the account of his great experience of discovering that David is the eternal son of the father. He wanted to write something which would prepare the reader for what was coming. The gist of it is this. He said, "What happened to me goes beyond any reasonable explanation in this world. It was through revelation, it could never be discovered by the reasoning mind, it had to be revealed". He goes on to say that he found it a burden, because he didn't know what to do with it. He said that the I am of man is Jesus, the Lord. His eternal son is David, and this is the experience that everyone has in store in this world. He ended the introduction by saying, "I now present my two witnesses. The internal witness of my experience, and the external witness of scripture".

I'm sure you're not surprised that Neville announced his coming death in the form of a joke. Remember I saw him looking like the Joker in my vision. This day, Halloween, probably the second or one of the two most joyous holidays in our calendar; Halloween and Christmas. Everyone seems to have a ball on both of these days. Now this day, Halloween, is a remnant, a modern day leftover from the most ancient religion in the world. We know that the Christian religion is true, but none of you would be here today if you believed now what you were taught when you were a child. Your eyes were opened, you're a privileged few to have had this revelation. Pope Leo the 10th, who was the son of Lorenzo Medicci, who was called Lorenzo the Magnificant because he was the great patron of art in the 15th century. This Pope Leo the 10th was pope at the very beginning of the 16th century. You see how long that is after the beginning of Christianity. Listen to what this man said, the pope, "What profit hath not that fable of Christ brought us?" Now the word profit means gain. "What profit hath not that fable of Christ brought us?" He's telling you that the religion as it was interpreted and handed down was a myth, that it never was history.

Saint Augustine, who helped save the Roman Catholic church at the time of the decline of Rome, he helped save the church by formulating a workable theology. He is the one who formulated the trinity. He had this to say, "That which is known as the Christian religion existed among the ancients and never did not exist from the very beginning of the human race". Now that religion he was talking about is the Egyptian myth of Osiris and the Egyptian religion of resurrection. You see, that is the story of Christianity, resurrection. That is what Neville experienced, he was resurrected and he told the story. He found

85

it in scripture in a way that could never be found until it was revealed.

The story of Osiris is this, this god king through treachery was induced to lie down in a big chest, a coffin. After he was in it, they closed it. They got him in it by the ruse, "Will you try it out? Will you see if you fit in it?" So he did, and they closed the lid and killed him. Then his body was dismembered, it was cut up into fragments, then these fragments were strewn all over the land of Egypt. Then his wife, Isis, reassembled the body as a mummy. She did all of this in the city called Anu in Egypt. While his body was lying there in this mummified form, his son, Horus, came to the mouth of the cave where he was lying and called into the cave and said, "Lord Asar, come forth". The ancient name is Asar. That is when Asar was resurrected. This religion is pre-historic, there are traces of it found all over the world on this continent and on the other continents.

In the gospel of John, the 11th chapter, you find the story of the resurrection of Lazarus in Bethany by Jesus. This story is a mutilation and a rescript of this ancient tale of Osiris. It comes from the Egyptian *Book of the Dead* and this book is thousands and thousands of years old. When the story was recast into Hebrew, when Horus calls to Asar and calls him Lord Asar, the Hebrew word for lord or god is used and that word is el. It's very much like the Spanish article el. So, he addressed him as El Asar. To the city Anu was added the Hebrew word beth, which means house. Anu in Egyptian meant the place of the multiplying bread. That town became Bethanu, and in time it converted into Bethany, which is the town in the gospel account, it was lifted right out of this Egyptian *Book of the Dead*. In the course of time, El Asar converted to Lazarus. The E wore off, the S changed to Z and a suffix, us, was added, so it became Lazarus. The mummy is connected with this religion, this cult, because Osiris, Asar, was the god of the dead in the underworld. For that reason, he was depicted as a mummy.

To the initiated in this religion, remember this sounds like a really trumped up myth, but this is the religion of the mind that build the great pyramid. You must look for another meaning or dismiss it altogether. The mind that built the great pyramid was an astonishing mind and this was their way of presenting the great mystery. To the initiated in this religion, the underworld is not an afterlife. The underworld is this world right here, this present day world, because God died when he came into this world. They understood this mystery that God fell asleep when he came down into this story of the play. The mummy represents the body, because the body is the coffin of the soul. My body is my coffin, I'm a prisoner here, I can't get out of it. As Neville said, "Even if you commit suicide, you simply go to another segment of time", according to his visions. You're restored to life immediately, we are prisoners of this world. This was their way of presenting the mystery of the incarnation, being imprisoned in this world.

Now this name, Asar, appears in the Hebrew language as various other words. You have the beginning of a pun, and we all love puns. Even a little child can understand a pun. The word asar in Hebrew is the word for 10. So you have not only the 10 commandments, you have the asar commandments. The word for maker in Hebrew is asa. Now you know New Englanders drop their Rs, so that shouldn't be any problem. You hear them saying power, so you know that an R had disappeared there. Asa is the maker. The Lord is our maker. The Lord is our asa. Your maker is your husband, asa is your husband. Here is this mystery concealed, of all places, in the Hebrew language. Now you remember that the Hebrew people, the children of Israel, came out of slavery in Egypt and they were led by a man named Moses. Moses was raised in the palace of Pharaoh himself. I'm not making this up, it's in scripture, it's been there thousands of years. Moses, living in the palace of Pharaoh spoke Egyptian. He got the best education of the day, he understood the mystery of the religion, therefore he could not possibly have been unaware of the pun play on the name Asar in the

Hebrew language.

A week after I gave my first lecture, I got a call from a friend of mine who was at the first lecture. He said, "Frank, the day of your lecture, that night I had a dream, and I want you to hear it. In my dream, the depth of my being was rejoicing, because I had found a monumental and glorious truth.

When I was fully awake I couldn't bring back anything concrete, all I could bring back was the glorious feeling of this truth". In the next part of the dream, he found himself on the sidewalk standing in front of Bullock's department store. There in front of Bullock's department store an information center concerning Neville was being constructed. He said, "It wasn't finished". He could see the super structure on which a round dome would eventually rest. Nevertheless very definitely there in front of Bullock's was this information center concerning Neville. Then a great argument arose, because this information center concerning Neville was obstructing the display case of the department store, and that was not appreciated. At that point, the center was moved immediately across the street, and then everything seemed to be alright. He said, 'I wonder what this means? I especially wonder why Bullock's? It was so definitely Bullock's". Now you know that a bullock is a young bull.

In my dream, my vision of Neville's death, he was standing in front of a restaurant. It was at that point that he choked and he turned blue in the face and fell back and all his bowels gushed out. The name of that restaurant was The Golden Bull. In my account at my first lecture, did not include the name of the restaurant. So you see the depth of his being disclosed a detail in this eternal story which I had simply passed over. Now the bull is the symbol of Osiris. I told you earlier that evidences of Osiris worship occur all over the Earth, and at these places they have discovered evidence of the worship of the bull. We still have sacred cows in India. Another feature of the cult of

88

Asar or Osiris is witchcraft, magic, it was practiced. What built the great pyramid would be the ability to use one's imagination to get whatever one wanted in this world. To someone who did not understand that principle, this would be witchcraft, this would be magic. This is what Neville taught, imagining creates reality. Out of that dream came this revelation, this symbol, the bull.

When the children of Israel were in the wilderness, Moses left them and went up on the high mountain to commune with God. The children of Israel lost their faith because they couldn't see anything in sight, then they urged Aaron to make them the golden calf. They had just come out of Egypt and they remembered the golden calf, the sign, the symbol of Osiris. So he made them the golden calf and they worshiped it. On the level of a parable, this is the worship of anything external. Neville, our guide, told us don't look to anything on the outside, it's all within you, it's all in your imagination.

Paul, who apparently was the founder of the Christian religion, especially gentiles who came into the Christian religion, tells us on the printed page in the form of a pun that he is Osiris. He is Asar. Listen to his words. At the very beginning of the Letter of Philemon Paul says, "I, Paul, a prisoner of Jesus Christ". In that short opening he reveals a secret. You know that Paul was bilingual, Paul spoke Hebrew and Greek. The word for prisoner in Hebrew is asir, and that word asir comes from the word asar, which means to bind. This is the mummy's condition. The mummy is bound, the mummy is the bound one in the underworld, the dead one in the underworld. He is telling you that he is Asar, that he has had the experience of resurrection, because he certainly wouldn't be rejoicing in the fact that he was still bound. He's telling you that he had the experience of resurrection. Now you know that Neville constantly compared his experiences with Paul. He did everything but say, "I am Paul". Paul was on the page, Neville was in history. There isn't anyone here who could doubt the fact that Neville Goddard was in this world and told his story.

Listen to Paul's telling you that he is Neville. In the second letter of Corinthians, the 12th chapter, the

11th verse, Paul makes this statement, "I am become a fool in glorying". The word for fool in Hebrew is nbl. You can hear that is a play on the name Neville. It is spelled in Hebrew N-B-L. There are no vowels in the Hebrew language. In Hebrew, B and V are interchangeable sounds, like in the Spanish language, we are so aware of Spanish here because our city is practically half Spanish speaking. You can't go anywhere without hearing the Spanish language here, and in that language B and V are interchangeable. So that name, Nbl, can be pronounced Nvl, which is a play on Neville. Now we have here two statements by Paul. One that he is Asar, two that he is Neville. The basic meaning of the word nbl is skin bag. This is where we come in. What better description could you give of the human body than that it is a skin bag? As a matter of fact, I saw a book by a dermatologist, either he had considered calling it the bag you live in or he did actually title his book *The Bag You Live In*. We are in a skin bag. The word for fool in English comes from the Latin word follies, which means wind bag. What more perfect description? A skin and a wind bag, that's us. Yet we are called by these two names, Neville and Asar, but it's all about us. It's in terms of these two characters, the one mythical and the other historical, because I must insist that Neville is historical, I shook his hand. Now we have these two names; Neville, Asar connected.

In the Old Testament in the Hebrew is an instrument called the neville asar. Another meaning of Neville is harp, and another meaning of asar is the instrument of 10 strings. The scholars admit they don't really know what this instrument is. In the 144th Psalm are these words, "Oh, God, I will sing a new song to you on the neville asar". The English translation of these two words in the King James, you can read it for yourself when you get home, the 144th Psalm, I don't know the verse, it's translated in the King James version as soltury, which is an old English term for a musical instrument, soltury, an instrument of 10 strings. Back here in the Psalms, this mystery has been concealed for thousands of years.

As I said before, today is the day of Halloween. This day is a remnant from the ancient cult of Osiris, because in their rituals to enact the truth, they put animal skins and put them on and they took animal's faces and put them on as masks. This day has come down as a traditional holiday. I'm sure it's equally as popular as Christmas, because everyone has such a great time. It's the day of magic, and Neville appeared as the magician. It's the day of mystery, because Paul told us that great is the mystery of our religion. He didn't tell you what that mystery was, he simply talked about it. This is the day of masquerade, and you can see that we're all here in a costume drama. We're all wearing the false face, because this is not your true being, and this was Neville's message.

Now are there any questions?

Audience Member 1: When you said Judas betrayed the Messianic **[inaudible 00:55:21]** go over that a little bit by explaining **[inaudible 00:55:25]**?

Frank: Yes, she wants to know what I meant by Judas betrayed the Messianic secret. It has several parts to it. The great Messianic secret is that David is the eternal son of God. Neville betrayed that, or another meaning of the word betray is revealed, he revealed it. The very name Judah comes from the hand, yod, which means the open hand, to reveal. Another part of the Messianic secret is that he revealed the hiding place of Jesus. Neville told us that Jesus is your own wonderful human imagination. No one here knew that until Neville came along and told them, so that was another revelation where Jesus was hiding. He's hiding in your skull. Does that clear it up? Did you think of your question, Harry?

91

Harry: Could you by any chance give that quotation that you gave about the pope, can you tell where from?

Frank: I got it from one of the two books I absolutely lean on, the scholarship in these books is unbelievable. The book is called *Who Is This King of Glory* and it's by Alvin Boyd Kuhn.

Harry: Could you say that again, please?

Frank: *Who Is This King of Glory*, Alvin Boyd Kuhn.

Harry: What's the other one?

Frank: *The Lost Light* by the same author. Any other questions?

Audience Member 2: [inaudible 00:58:24]

Frank: Yes. These are states of consciousness. Neville had all the experiences of scripture, he said that so many times from the platform. He said, "I have experienced scripture from beginning to end, I have experienced all of the states in scripture. This is all a parable, so we have different names. In that Letter of Philemon, which is very short, Paul mentions the bowels four times. Since the letter is so short, he had to be telling a mystery. When you read that letter, the word bowels just jumps up and hits you in the face, because you're not expecting it. Here again is a connection between Paul and Judas, because Paul in this letter mentions the bowels and it's Judas who spills his bowels. Any other questions? I love you for coming.

[01:00:11] [END OF AUDIO]

Frank Carter Lecture 6: Dated 11/7/76

Male Speaker 1: November 7th, 1976. The lecturer is Frank Carter.

Frank Carter: Last week, I began the lecture by telling you on the way over here I heard on the radio, that this Halloween was the 50th anniversary of the death of Harry Houdini, the great magician. Then, I went on to tell you the devil appeared as a magician in my vision of him. Just before he departed, I had the vision of Neville as Judas. And, he was dressed as a magician and his face was ashen white, like the joker in Batman. It was so vivid. Then, he fell back, and all of his bowels gushed out.

Now, this is the description of the death of Judas in the first chapter of Acts. When I discovered that this was in Acts, that I had had this experience, I called him. He told me that the vision was true. Then, Neville departed in exactly the same way and I saw his body. So, this is my authority for telling this story. Otherwise, I would not be standing here, I would be playing the piano, I am a musician. Now, Harry Houdini, was The Great Escape Artist. And, so was Neville, The Great Escape Artist, because he told us that he was going to depart this world for good.

He explained that this is a play here. This is the whirl of the wheel. Woodland, as Blake called it. And, he said beyond any question of doubt, he was going to escape this world. You might say that he discovered the fatal flaw in this world. He discovered that this world is not what it appears to be, that we are not the beings which we think we are. That we are actually God the Father, here in a masquerade. In a play. Neville, did everything but tell us that he was the character, Paul.

Now, you know that Paul is for all intents and purposes, the founder of the Christian religion, because he was really the one who got the religion started among the gentiles. Paul talks about the great

93

mystery of the religion, but he never really comes out and explains the mystery, he simply expounds it. Now, Paul and Neville had the identical experiences. Many a time on the platform, Neville said, "I can say with Paul, that I have run the course, and the time of my departure cannot be far off".

Now, beyond the fact that they had the identical experiences, there is concealed, in scripture itself, the name, Neville. In connection with the character, Paul. Listen to Paul's words. In second Corinthians, the 12th chapter, the 11th verse, Paul says this. "I am become of fool in glorying". Now, Paul was bilingual. He spoke Hebrew, and Greek fluently. So, he was well aware of double meanings, of puns. The word of fool in Hebrew is [foreign word] you can hear that this is a play on Neville.

In another place, the particular place escapes me right now, he says when he is talking about the Lord's supper, and the Lord's body, that he will make everything clear when he comes. Now, apparently, this letter was written to the Corinthians. Nevertheless, he is saying to the reader, that he will make everything clear when he comes. And, in this other place he has said, "I have become, Neville". And, we know that they had the identical experiences.

This summer, right after I finished my series, I promptly went out and broke my wrist ice skating. You know the old wish, break an arm and a leg, well, I did it. When I was in the doctor's office waiting for my appointment, I chanced upon the old Saturday Evening Post. I did not know that they had resumed publication. But, it was the September issue of the Saturday Evening Post. So, I was looking through it, and I found the most fascinating story. That was where I got the term, 'Fatal flaw'.

This, apparently, is a true story. It is about an orphan, who probably at this point, is in his early 20's. He was a chess genius. At age five, he was playing chess at chess club in New York City. He had the nickname 'Poop'. Poop Glover was his name. He got his nickname because he had a habit of saying, "Poop", just before he checkmated his opponent. Now, for a long time, no-one understood, because he said it about five moves before the check mate. In other words, this genius knew that five moves before, he was going to checkmate his opponent.

Now, I know nothing about the game of chess, I hope later when we have questions, if there is someone here who is knowledgeable about chess, they will discuss this. He played chess from about the time of five to eight years of age. Then, he was taken in to the home of relatives, and so he dropped out of sight. But, he suddenly quit playing chess, and no-one understood why. The author of this story tracked down his relatives, and discovered that the boy one day said, "Chess, no good".

The boy was not good at communicating. He was a genius at chess, but he practically could not express himself. He said, "Chess, no good". Then, they got out of him, that he had discovered the flaw in the game of chess. And, he showed his relative how, within a very few moves at the beginning of the game, he could prevent any manoeuvre on the opponents' part. And, it did not matter who started the game. Think about it. This game is centuries old. It's almost a sub-culture.

Volumes of books have been written about this game, about the intricacies of this game, and along comes a child and discovers the flaw that it is no longer what it had been believed to be. So, he discovered the fatal flaw. And so, did Neville. He discovered the fatal flaw in this world. This is not the reality we think it to be. That we came into this world as in a masquerade, and he told us that we were going to have the same experience that he had, of awakening from this dream.

Now, he had his experience by seeing David. David, in The Old Testament appeared to him and called him Father. Then, he knew, without a shadow of a doubt, we are in a play here. Now, in The Old Testament, in first Samuel, the 25th chapter is a complete parable about this experience. But, it is told in a way that could never be understood until it actually happened. I told you that Paul revealed himself as Nabal. When Paul is Nabal The Fool, he is telling you, as a mystery, that he had the experience of seeing his son David.

And, this is what happened to the Neville we knew. He was actually here in history, his voice is on tapes. It's not a matter of hearsay, there are books left which he wrote. So, we know that this man was in history, we know he had that experience because he told us. And now, he has departed and we see now that his name was actually in scripture. That is the theme of my lectures, scripture, Neville, and you. Because it is all about you. A man named Neville came into history to explain what was written in scripture 2,000 years ago.

Probably longer. Then, he departed. Then. this mystery of his name in scripture was revealed. Some year before he departed, I saw him one night, in a dream, dressed as a jester. He had on ca and bells, and he was dressed in a tutu, you know, the ballet costume, and he was dancing across the stage. Like a soft shoe dance. Now, you know that Neville was actually a dancer in Vaudeville? He had the most idiotic grin on his face, he looked absolutely ridiculous. Well, you know, Neville was such a dignified man, I did not want to tell him.

But, that is the thing about these dreams, these visions. They are often so strange, so funny that you are tempted to dismiss them. But, I told him anyway, and he was delighted beyond measure. He did not say anything, he just smiled when I said, "I saw you as the fool". After he departed, I had this dream one night. In my dream, I saw a friend of mine who is named, David. So, you could day that in one sense, I saw my friend, but in another sense, I found David, because I ran into David.

Then, as I was leaving my friend, Neville suddenly appeared and grabbed me by the shoulders, and kissed me on the cheek, and disappeared immediately. I thought, "What's this?" Then, after I got up, I went to my bible and I practically opened scripture to this story of

Nabal The Fool, in The Old Testament. Now, I am pronouncing it, 'Naval', as a 'V'. When you read it in scripture, you will see that it is spelled, N-A-B-A-L. As I have explained before, in the Hebrew language, there are no vowels.

It's like, the license plates on cars, you see consonants and you wonder, "What word that would spell". Also, in the Hebrew language, 'B', and 'V', are inter-changeable sounds, like the Spanish language. So, I am pronouncing it, "'Naval". In the story, Nabal is actually described as, The Fool, which is one of the few instances in scripture in which the text itself defines the meaning. Nabal is sheering his sheep. This was a big festival in the ancient world.

Now, David and his men had been in the wilderness where Nabal's men had been, and David and his men had defended Nabal's men from outlaws, had kept them safe. So, when David heard that Nabal was sheering his sheep, he set work to Nabal and he said, "We have protected your men, and this is the time of the festival, lots of eating and drinking. Can you send us provisions? Food, drink?" And, he ends his supplication by saying, "If you can do this for your son, David".

David calls Nabal, 'Father', by saying that he is his son. Now, instead of responding, Nabal The Fool, sends back word, "Who is David? And who is the son of Jessie?", and he goes on to say, "There be many slaves, servants these days, that have broken away from their masters". He is very insulting. But, notice what he said, he says, "Who is David?", and, "Who is the son of Jessie?" So here, in this parable form, between the lines is concealed this mystery. The Fool is finding out that David is his son.

But, it is told in this parable form, in this dramatic way. Just as I saw Neville as Judas, as the bad guy. But, it turns out like in the **[unintelligible 00:18:03]** that the one upon whom the suspicion is cast, is not the culprit. When David hears what Nabal says, he swears to avenge himself. In the meantime, one of the young men goes to Nabal's wife, who is named, Abigail, and tells her what is about to happen. And so, she intervenes. She goes, with provisions, to David.

While she was going, scripture tells us, "She rode on the ass". Now, you know that the ass is the symbol of the body, Neville explained this very definitely. When she meets David, she falls down before him and says, "Don't talking your vengeance out on my husband Nabal, he is a fool". And so, she herself says that he is a fool. Then she says, "Nabal is his name, and folly is with him". Now you know, that a man's life has nothing in scripture, has nothing to do with sex on this level.

In scripture, a man's wife means the emanation, the soul, the personality. You might say that when two people stand talking, you see two people, but when they converse, they must meet on a mental level. Otherwise, there is no way to communicate. And so, this emanation coming out between two people, is the wife. So, here we have the mystery of the one being whose wife is named Abigail. Now, in Hebrew, Abigail means, 'Father of Joy'.

So, when Abigail saw David, David saw his father, because the name Abigail means, 'Father of Joy'. David said, "Blessed be the Lord God of Israel who sent you to me this day". That was his response to Abigail. Again, we have the mystery of the outer and the inner man. Nabal is the outer man, because you know that the basic meaning for Nabal in Hebrew is, 'Skin Bag'. What better description of the human body? It is a skin bag. And, that name is Nabal, Neville.

You see, it's your name too. Because, in Hebrew philosophy, Hebrew thought, the name described the nature of things. So, when you look at the outer man, you are looking at the skin bag. It's the husk the holds the grain. The inner man, is the being you really are. That is Abigail, Father of Joy. Now, Neville was the one who discovered this, and then he told us. And, the story itself is told in terms of his name. Now, you know that when he was only a few days old, his mother

98

was wondering what to name the child.

She heard a voice say, "His name, is Neville". She looked around, there was no-one. About that time, his uncle walked up the stairs and she said, "Did you say anything?", and he said, "No. But the baby's name is Neville". So, you see, his name was assigned. Because, the [foreign word] knew that this man, Neville, was the one who was going to reveal the fatal flaw to the characters here in this story. You might say he blew the whistle on the whole thing.

He told us, he said, "It's not at all what you think it is. We are sound asleep here. But, we have this experience in store so that we can depart this world and go back". As he did. He is our guide. And you know, Judas, was described as the guide to them that took Jesus. Now, that word 'took', can be interpreted to, 'who accepted. Who believed'. He guided us to the hiding place of Jesus, he said, "Jesus is not a character in scripture. Jesus is your own, wonderful, human imagination".

And, it's literally true in scripture, what he believed. I saw Neville dressed as a magician, with a cape. Now, a cape is a covering, just as this body we are wearing is a garment. The garment of flesh. So, the symbolism, the literal symbolism right down the line, is fabulous, but it is all concealed there in scripture. Now, Paul and Neville, as I said, had identical experiences. When Paul appears in scripture, his name is, Saul, and he is a very dedicated Jew. A zealot.

When this story of Christ came out, and the people were followers of the way. They were believing this new story, this new interpretation. He was among those who persecuted. So, in this sense, he was like Judas. It's all a parable, all of these clues are strewn out. But, you gather them one by one. He was present at the stoning of Stephen. He guarded the cloaks of those who were stoning Stephen. Then, Paul, on the way to Damascus, experienced the risen Lord.

He says later in another place, "Have I not seen the risen Lord?"

Now, when he had this experience of seeing the risen Lord, his name was changed to Paul. Neville's name was a sign from the very beginning. But, Paul's name was changed from Saul, to Paul. Now, Neville often said that King Saul, in The Old Testament, who persecuted David, was the same character as Saul in The New Testament, whose name was changed to Paul. Now, the name Paul, itself, in Hebrew, means 'maker'.

The Lord is you maker. You maker is your husband. Aside from being the word 'maker', a form of Paul is actually a name for the Hebrew verb. In another place we have, "The word was made flesh. The verb was made flesh". Paul is telling you, between the lines, in pur form, that he is the word made flesh. And, he was indeed the founder of the religion, he spread the religion. There was no record whatsoever in the ancient world. Paul was a character on the page, and Neville was a character in history.

He had the identical experiences with Paul. And so, I say he was Paul. But, so are we. Because, our real nature is the maker. We are the word. And, we became flesh. We became Nabal, the skin bag, the body. So, it sounds like at times we are talking about Neville, and perhaps extolling him, but the whole story is told in terms of his name. They had the same experiences. Paul in second Corinthians, 13th verse maybe first Corinthians, where he is speaking of love as the greatest thing in the world, he says, "Now, we look through a glass darkly".

But then, face to face. The word glass in Greek, means 'mirror'. Not a glass like a pane of glass, but a mirror. You know that there is only one reason why you look into a mirror, that is to see you face, otherwise, you cannot see your own face. He says, "We see now, through a mirror, but then we are going to see face to face". Neville had this experience, he told so often, his experience of seeing the large quartz. And, as he looked at it, it fragmented.

Then, it reassembled as his own glorified form, as Buddha in the lotus posture. And, he said he knew that he was seeing the being that he really is. So, here is Paul's experience. Then, the experience of the name, the change of name. The experience of being resurrected from the dead. Paul never comes out and actually says that he was resurrected, it's all hidden, it's all a mystery to be revealed when the man who is to have the experience comes into history, and tells it.

That is why I congratulate everyone here that they believed him, because it is a great gift to be able to believe what you cannot prove. But now, the proof has come, his credentials were concealed in scripture thousands of years ago. He came into history, came into the church, which had misinterpreted the story, changed it into history, in the interpretation. Came into this church, had his experience, and found that he could no longer believe what he had been taught.

No matter how much he loved those who had taught him the interpretation, he could no longer believe it, because he had found the truth. Are there any questions? Does anyone know anything about chess?

Male Speaker 4: You brought up a good question now, in my mind. And, I always wondered about it, I played chess. I have for years, but recently though it's hard to find anybody that had the time to sit down and really play chess. So, I can see now, with these different characters there undoubtedly is a mystery in the game of chess that has to do with the game of life itself, because of the different characters that are there. Especially the King and the Queen, and the little people as the pawns.

I am going to look into it a little bit further, I have got books on it too. But, I see now where they are interrelated, undoubtedly, into the particular mystery of life.

Frank: Yes. That is why when I read the story, I suddenly remembered how often Neville said that all of the volumes, or works written about the Christian religion, all of these discussions are based on a misinterpretation. Volumes of them.

Male Speaker 4: Chess is older than the Christian religion. I just want to thank you for explaining some of the things that were a little bit hard for me to understand even as Neville gave it at the time. Now, you are bringing some of these things up in a down to Earth explanation. I know he did not have the time to go into it in detail.

Frank: I know that he knew these things. I do not understand why he did not tell it.

Male Speaker 4: Well, it might have sounded egotistical.

Frank: Yes.

Female Speaker 1: He admired Blake so much. And, Blake always said you know **[inaudible 00:33:56]** I think he wanted us, the church, to say-- You know yourself, every time you would go back stage and talk to him about a dream or a vision you had, **[inaudible 00:34:09]**

Female Speaker 2: I felt really **[unintelligible 00:34:20]** Neville that he assumed that you knew. I think that was the-- I know that **[inaudible 00:34:29]** and he always explained it in terms that I could understand. But it's just as if it were-- If you try to define something that you do automatically, you **[unintelligible 00:34:50]**

Frank: Well, I do not mind telling you, I feel like I am getting to know you quite well. I attempted to tell a few people what I told you today, and they practically jumped down my throat.

Male Speaker 4: You know, Neville said that any time someone tries to take their Jesus away from them, or their God away from them, remember, it is not the true God. But, you cannot **[unintelligible 00:35:31]** everybody. I have been laughed at.

Frank: That is why I said that the size of the group is not important to me. The important things is that those who want to hear it, are here. And, I could not be more delighted, because I am getting it out of my system.

Female Speaker 2: The most strange thing, is the people that have got all the degrees, biology degrees and so on. They are the ones that become the most confused. We had a retired pastor in our organization, and I invited him to have a, your faith is your fortune, and he kept, he would watch it once, when he gave it back he was just, "I am totally confused".

Male Speaker 4: He never wanted the question brought up anymore, either. Because it was liable to take his Jesus away from him.

Female Speaker 1: All through the Bible, they often knew that they **[unintelligible 00:36:25]**

Frank: Can you imagine being wide awake in this world, as he was? He was too humble to set himself up, but there can be no question of doubt that he was wide awake, and here. So, I can see how he wanted to go. Because, so many times I had the privilege of driving him to the lectures when David Morton could not make it. So, many times, especially when Missus Goddard was ill, he would say, "All I want to do is get my sweetheart well, and then depart this world as quickly as possible". He said that so many times.

Male Speaker 4: The question that is always asked, why could he not have done anything for his wife? I tried to explain it to them the way Neville explained it, how she emulated her mother's own life until she became every bit of her, including the disease. It is hard for people to understand that, that if he was such a man and undoubtedly was powerful enough that he could have cured her. But, they misunderstand, just like the Bible is misinterpreted.

Frank: Well, you know that her recovery was miraculous. She had 20 operations, in two years. You know what a shock to the system even one operation is. One of the nurses, just a young girl with a wet slip, she said, "We seen pictures of you over at the hospital school. You're famous". Of course, she should not have told that but, the girl let it slip. None of them believed that she would recover, and yet she did.

Female Speaker 1: I think I told you at the house one night, about **[inaudible 00:39:21]**

Frank: I think I told that she fused with Neville. You know, that was Neville's first great experience. When he was taken in to the divine council one night, and he fused with infinite love, and that was the word she used. She said that she fused with Neville, there can be no doubt that very soon, she will be resurrected, she will have the experience. I have not had the experience. That is why I feel like I do not have anything to talk about except Neville's credentials, as thy are sealed in scripture. I believed him, I did not know why.

I used to kid him I would say, "You know, if I ever find anything better, I am leaving you". He said, "May I tell you that I hope that you do". Well, if there are no more questions, thank you for coming.

Male Speaker 4: **[inaudible 00:41:12] [unintelligible 00:41:18]** I go to the metaphysical section. On one of these occasions, I went to pick out a book, and another little book fell out on the floor. I picked the book up, and looked at it **[inaudible 00:41:39]** little old dirty book, and knew it was not anything **[inaudible 00:41:42]** I stuck it back in the shelf, took my book, and went off. When I returned the book, I went back to the metaphysical section to find a book, and this little book fell out again.

I put it back up again, but what had happened **[inaudible 00:41:55]** I took it home. About a week or so later, I did, there was a little picture of Neville in that little **[unintelligible 00:42:11]** and he was speaking, and I could not wait to tell him, "The guy that wrote this book, he is gonna speak. I wanna go hear him". **[END OF AUDIO]**

Frank Carter Lecture 7: Dated 11/14/76

Frank Carter: This book, a message that has never been heard before and as I've said before I congratulate all of you who are here not to hear me, but because you believed him.

Last week I talked about Neville the magician again because in my vision of Neville as Judas I saw him dressed as a magician standing in front of a restaurant. It was at that point that he choked, he turned blue in the face and he fell back. When he fell back on the sidewalk all of his bowels gushed out. This is recorded in the book of Acts in the first chapter.

I also mentioned that Harry Houdini who's 50th birthday was on Halloween was not only a great magician he was a great escape artist. Now Neville was a great escape artist too because he got out of this world of the story this world of the wheel because he had the experience of seeing his son David the eternal son David. At that point, I told you a short story which I read in the Saturday Evening Post, the September issue. Now the story was told as if it were a true story.

It was about a boy genius who was so good at chess that he began playing at the age of five then he quit when he was around eight years of age and they discovered that this boy had discovered a fatal flaw in chess. He had discovered that he could keep his opponents from winning by making a series of about five moves at the very beginning of the game thereby circumventing any strategy which his opponent might try to use. Now this boy at this point would be about 20 years of age, now he has to make the decision whether he is going to reveal this secret or whether he will go on to use the secret to become wealthy because undoubtedly, he would become the greatest chess player in the world.

Now whether this story is true or not really doesn't matter, if it's not true it's a parable, but everything in this world is a parable. It's all about you because you wrote the book before you came in and now you're in this mystery. I told the story which is found in the first book of Samuel the 25th Chapter. This is a complete parable of the meeting between Nevale the fool and David his eternal son. As I pointed out its told in the form of a parable so that you could never discover the meaning until this story became true, in other words because history.

Now there is a fatal flaw in history. The western church won't admit it but judging by their words and their actions they took the ancient scriptures the ancient allegories and turned them in to history. Now you all know who Martin Luther is, the Roman Catholic Church had been all powerful from about the beginning of Christianity. You know there was a struggle in the early church. That struggle boils down to the controversy about whether scripture was history or whether it was allegory. Now if you heard that the iron curtain had been purchased it was going to be moved to Havasu City to keep company with the London Bridge you wouldn't believe it for one minute because you know that the iron curtain is an allegory.

Martin Luther made the first translation in to the common tongue of the people, that language was German. 1922 when it came out after intervention of the printing press it was possible. Now when he made his translation he had a great deal of trouble because he had to take the picturesque language which came from the Egyptian this language was allegorical it came from the Egyptian it was then recast in to Hebrew it was then recast in to Greek then there was a Latin translation later. So, he had to invent practically a whole new series of word pictures to fit the language he was attempting to translate.

Now the Pope at that time when Luther nailed his 95 thesis supposedly on the door of the church in Wittenberg that Pope was Leo the 10th. Now listen to what this man said, "What prophet hath not that fable of Christ brought us" Now that word prophet means gain, in other words they were becoming wealthy because of the fable that they had used to enslave the people. Now Martin Luther objected to the sale of indulgences, in other words the forgiveness of sins.

When the people wanted to have their sins forgiven or when they wanted to be released from a few days in purgatory or hell they paid a certain sum of money. Now the point I'm making is that Luther stood up to the church but at the same time he didn't say anything about the fable. His point was this in reading the letters of Paul he had come upon the doctrine of justification by faith, in other words you don't earn your grace it's all a gift it's all revealed.

So, you see he stood up to the church then came the split Protestantism was formed but only the religion as it was interpreted had split there was no new revelation, even Luther who could read scripture wasn't aware of the fact that this was a fable. Now modern scholars generally agree that the religion which was set up by Jesus and his disciples as the story is recorded in the Gospels and in Acts that that religion would not have lasted one generation, it would have died out. Now the man who was responsible for preserving this faith was Paul. There is every indication that Paul was an initiate of the mystery schools.

These schools flourished in ancient Egypt they spread in to Greece. So what Paul did was take the substance of this esoteric doctrine and bury it in scripture in his letters. Now the interesting thing about this is that a lot of people object to this statement they say, "Oh no that isn't" I'm talking about that fundamentalists now, they say, "Oh no that isn't the religion. I know that isn't the religion I believe in" and yet here it is buried in scripture.

Now Paul never really reveals what the mystery is, he talks about the mystery of Christ. Now he was the first one really to discuss the mystery of Christ because if you read the Gospels you find the story mainly about this central character who is called Jesus. Now you know as Neville told us that Jesus is the I am of every person in this world, there is only one being in the whole world and that name is I am. Nevertheless, we are wearing these garments of flesh. Now this is the mystery that Paul was concealing the mystery of Christ in you.

Last week I told the parable from the first book of Samuel the 25th Chapter about the meeting between David who is the Christ and the Neval the fool who is his father and didn't even know it. This is what Neville told us that he had that experience that never in a million years would he have dreamed that this story was buried in scripture and that he was the eternal father of this eternal son David and he felt that he was commissioned to tell it and so he did tell it.

Now I also told you last week how Paul identifies himself. He says in second Corinthians the 12 Chapter the 11th Verse, "I am become a fool in glorying" now the word for fool in Hebrew is Neval it's a play on the name Neville, Neval. So, Paul is telling you that he is Neville. Now Neville is who you are because you are wearing this garment of flesh. The word Neval is the word for skin bag and this is a perfect description of the human body. So, you see while you're here in this world you are actually called after the name of the one who revealed the secret to you.

Now you know in Hebrew thought the name for a thing is its nature. The name describes what the nature of that thing is and so when you look at the body it's a skin bag and so it is named Neval. This is your own body because when you speak of your body you would say the body is the means by which I am in the world but your eternal name is I am. We appear to be different beings but actually we are one being. I am standing up here talking to you, you are sitting listening and while we are here on this level we can't see that we are one being, there is only one being in this room and yet we are partitioned off in these bodies.

Now in the first letter of Corinthians the 11th Chapter Paul discusses the Lords Supper in the course of this discussion he says that he is going to tell us, no remember this is for us the reader that's who scripture is addressed to the reader, he says he is going to tell us something he received from the Lord himself and then he goes on to say that the Lord Jesus the night in which he was betrayed took bread and broke it and said, "here take this, this is my body". Likewise, after supper he took the cup and he said, "Take this and drink it this is my blood of the new covenant".

Now Paul is telling you that he received this from the Lord Jesus himself. Then he goes on to explain a few more things and he ends the chapter by saying that he will clear everything up when he comes. Now an orthodox Christian would say, "Well this letter was written to the Corinthians. He was talking to the Corinthians" but he wasn't he was addressing this to the reader and remember it was the church that made the mistake of turning allegory in to history and after they did that it was a blood bath.

We've had 16 centuries of darkness in the western world and it all dates from the time in Judaism and the beginning of Christianity when these ancient secret writings were revealed to the public at large and misinterpreted and turned in to history and yet it is literally true. It's literally true as an experience for the most high, now remember you are the most high because you say I am and you are the most high because you are able to look at the little marks on the paper and read the meaning.

Only the most high can do this it's as if we're lying asleep in the pages reading and then all of a sudden comes a revelation and why I'm readying about myself. How do I know that? How do I know this is true? Because a man named Neville appeared in history demonstrated that he had had all of Paul's experiences. I told you he saw his own being as God. He tells you he was resurrected from the dead but it's in a veiled form because the mystery of the resurrection comes from Egypt from

109

ancient Egypt and it was the God Osiris whose name Assar was the one who was resurrected from the dead by his son Horus. Now one of the attributes of Horus was the eternal youth and David was personified as the eternal youth.

But all of this was hidden until the time when it would be revealed. Comparative religion has shown there are 180 points of similarity between Horus, who was the son of Osiris Assar, 180 points of similarity between Horus and the character Jesus in the Gospels. Now these writing, these Egyptian writings were already venerable with age in 3,500 BC, 3,500 years before this supposed event took place. Now at this point I'd like to tell you another story by Jorge Luis Borges who was one of Neville's favorite authors. This man is still living, he lives in Argentina. I think he is in his 70's now.

Is it too warm for anyone in here? Fine.

He lives in Argentina and he begins this story which is called The Book of Sand S-A-N-D. He begins it by quoting from Herbert who was a mystic poet, Neville often quoted this man. I believe he wrote the verse my soul I heard today that none doth build a stately mansion but he who means to dwell therein. I believe this man wrote that.

Now beginning the story is a quotation from Herbert simply your rope of sand. Your rope of sand. He goes on to say that a line is made up of an infinite number of points. A plain is made up of an infinite number of lines. Volume is made up of an infinite number of plains. The hyper-volume is made up of an infinite number of hyper-volumes and then he stops and he says, "No talking in geometrical terms is not the best way to begin my story, but I assure you that my story is true".

Then he tells that one night a man comes to his door and he is selling bibles. The man is from the Orkney Islands off of Scotland and the man telling the story say, "Why I have about 10 bibles in the house" he said, "I even have the Wycliffe Bible which is the first translation in

110

English" and he goes, "I also have the Luther translation which is well-known to be the most unsatisfactory from a standpoint of literature" the man says, "Well I have something else I want to sell you" and he shows him a book and on the spine of the book is written Holy Scripture Holy Writ and underneath that Bombay.

He says, "I bargained with an outcast in India for this book. He felt it was the book of the Devil and he wanted to get rid of it so I exchanged this book for a bible. I gave him a bible" and he says, "No examine it" so he opens the book and looks at a page and sees a smudgy little drawing of an anchor much like a schoolboy would draw and the man says take a good look at it because you will never see it again and so he decides to test this so he closes the book and marks the spot opens it up and he can't find it and he notices that the left hand page is numbered 999 and the right hand page is numbered with a number to the 27th power.

In other words, they don't match and so the man who has brought the book says, "Now try to find the beginning of the book, the first page" So he opens the book and he tries to turn the first page and before he can get anywhere a number of leaves fill in so that he can't find the first page and he says, "Now try to find the last page" and the same thing happens before he can come to the page other pages come in and take the place. So, they bargained for this book and he gives him the Wycliffe Bible which was priceless and his pension check for the month.

Over the ensuing days and months and years he loves his book so much, he spends all of his time with it. He catalogues the appearances of the images which he can never find again, the book is infinite. He said he was slightly given to being a loner anyway and this made him a complete loner because he wanted to guard his book then is occurs to him that this is a monstrous book and that he can be no less monstrous himself for harboring a book like this. So, he thinks perhaps he should burn it and he thinks, "No if I should set fire to an infinite book then the world itself would be filled with infinite smoke".

So, then he knows what he will do. He used to work in the library in Buenos Aries and so one day quickly he slips in the front door makes a fast right turn down the stairs to where he knows that the maps and periodicals are, takes great care not to see exactly where he puts it and loses the book of sand of the dusty shelves and that's the end of the tale.

Now I mentioned the magician earlier. This story came out of Egypt. Moses who brought the children of Israel out of Egypt, now you know he was not a character but that doesn't matter we are in a parable, he was not historical in that sense, but he was raised in the palace of Pharaoh himself. He had the best education of the day, he spoke both Egyptian and Hebrew. He had access to the ancient writings In the court of Pharaoh, we know from reading the story in Genesis were magicians as a matter of fact they were able to duplicate all of the miracles which Moses and Aaron performed to try and get Pharaoh to let the people go.

Now the secret teaching of the mystery school was magic. I explained in an earlier lecture to someone who didn't understand the principle that imagining creates reality this principle applied would appear to be magic because all of us who have followed Neville who have use his teachings know that the principal works. That you can have anything in this world you want through imagining.

Now this was taught in these mystery schools so here was the magic, here's the magician because this was Neville's first theme.

He was sent out to teach and so he taught imagining creates reality he taught it for years. Had an audience of thousands. Then he experienced the promise which itself is buried is concealed in this very story of imagining creates reality. So, he started teaching that, after that there were those who simply could not receive it and they fell away and

112

those of us that are left who are able to receive this story of the promise.

Now to show that the New Testament is lifted from the ancient writings Neville often used the illustration which the central character would use when he was talking about faith that if you want something believe that you have already received it and you will receive it. Now Neville was the only person who ever explained that satisfactory for me. I remember reading it when I was a child but I didn't know how to use it and then I found Neville and he said, "The explanation of this saying is to use your imagination" and when he said that I said, "Well yes that's so clear. That's exactly what you do. You imagine that you have already received it".

Now in two places the central character equates the one who imagines with God. In one place someone says, "Will you do this for me if you can?" and the central character say, "If it's possible, all things are possible to him who believes". So, there is one statement. In another place, he makes the statement all things are possible to God, so he's equating the one who believes with God the one who is able to use his imagination is God. This is what Neville taught.

So, we have Neville who came to deliver this message after he departed it became clear that his very name is buried in scripture is concealed in scripture, now for what reason? To show that what he was telling was the truth because I always believed him. I didn't know why. I used to tell him I said, "I don't know why I believe you but I do. I don't have one shred of evidence that what you're telling me is the truth" and he [unintelligible 00:33:59]. So then when he departed as Judas that was the key which opened up these scriptures which had been concealed for untold centuries.

Paul makes a statement that this secret, this mystery of Christ was hidden from the ages. Now he's undoubtedly saying there that even the members of the mystery schools the most enlightened minds of their times did not know did not understand what was coming. They preserve the mystery they preserve the rituals but they didn't even know what was coming. So, you see what a parable this is because the man actually came in to the world.

Paul told in that letter of first Corinthians that he will clear everything up when he comes and so in to the world he came and yet even though its told in terms of his own name there is no possible way whatsoever to deify him because his message was that it's all about you it's simply told in terms of his name and his experience and this is a parable for you for your imagination because it reveals you to yourself as the most high because you are able to understand this mystery and that's the proof because you wrote the story. Cast yourself in this play and now you're in the act of waking.

Now are there any questions?

Male speaker 1: [unintelligible 00:36:23]. Female speaker 1: Excuse me.

Frank Carter: Yes.

Female speaker 1: This book that you are referring to The Book of Sand is it available [unintelligible 00:36:41].

Frank Carter: I read this story in the New Yorker magazine. Sometimes I think maybe that I almost feel that magazine is my catalog of images my personal catalog of images because I ran in to the story, the other one, last summer when I started these lectures and it fit right in with what I was telling. As I said we're in a parable every minute in this world is a parable.

So, there was a story in the magazine which I could use and just before I began on Halloween I thought wouldn't it be wonderful if another story appeared and there it was in the Halloween issue. I didn't know how I would use it but I knew that it would be used and incidentally this was Neville's and Bills favorite magazine, they could

114

hardly wait for the New Yorker to arrive. I'm not selling the magazine, but it's in the New Yorker. Yes?

Male speaker 2: Neville one time quoted another poem that was written by this author and I've tried on numerous occasions to find his works now his works are originally written in the Spanish language.

Frank Carter: Some are in-

Male speaker 2: And now they've been interpreted, but that particular one that he was talking about the book that poem was in-- I don't know how many times-- I've been in all kinds of stores and most of the libraries, can't find that particular one. Now I didn't know about this one here but I know not everything that he wrote is translated in to English but his works are available. In fact, he was featured here about a year ago in the Los Angeles Times.

Frank Carter: I didn't know that.

Male speaker 2: Yes, he's quite **[unintelligible 00:38:53].** He's quite a poet. He's a mystic, there is no if's or and's about it he is a mystic.

Frank Carter: Absolutely.

Male speaker 2: You just have to go around and search that's all.

Frank Carter: Right, probably-

Male speaker 2: If you have the spelling of his name you need that and I believe-

Female speaker 1: I just **[unintelligible 00:39:10]. Frank Carter:** B-O-R-G-E-S.

Female speaker 1: G-E what?

Frank Carter: G-E-S.

Male speaker 2: And there is an apostrophe between the E and the S.

Frank Carter: I don't believe so. No.

Male speaker 2: Well I could be wrong.

Frank Carter: Probably if you were to write the New Yorker they could tell you where his book--

Male speaker 2: It would be much better if you order a subscription at the same time.

[crosstalk]

Frank Carter: Any other questions?

Female speaker 2: You say all this an allegory but also Paul is an allegory **[unintelligible**

00:40:06] were allegories right all of **[unintelligible 00:40:10].**

Frank Carter: Right. Think of the word Paul itself, here's another pun in English. You know what a Paul is, it's a covering P-A-L-L, same sound. I don't want to stretch this too far but there is no coincidence in this world. I asked my mother when I was trying to explain some of this to her I got on this and I said, "Have you ever heard of a funeral pall?" and she said, "Oh my goodness yes. Why when I was a little girl in the south we used to have those things draped over the coffins and we knew what the funeral palls were".

As I've told before your body is your coffin it's your pall and Paul identifies himself as Neville. This is the mystery which came out of Egypt. They understood the incarnation and they cast it in to this vivid story. As Neville so often said, "If you want to get the point across tell a story" truth embodied in a tale shall enter in at lowly doors. How often he quoted that.

Female speaker 2: Could you say something-- you know this morning I was watching Saturday night television it was about the origin of the Mormon church Latter Day Saints **[unintelligible 00:41:46]** was talking about it he was saying Paul Smith that he was the founder-

Frank Carter: Joseph.

Female speaker 2: He's the founder of the church and was saying that as a boy he had a vision of where to find these tablets which he did and that's the basis of the religion. Okay now when they think that's not the truth and when actually it isn't as we know I mean its **[unintelligible 00:42:17]**.

Frank Carter: I don't understand Mormonism thoroughly but to me the tip off, always the tipoff is that they believe its history. That is the big giveaway.

Female speaker 2: I understand that but what I'm saying is the man that he found these tablets through a vision [crosstalk] his vision is not a true-- I mean his findings aren't the truth so **[unintelligible 00:42:56]**. Where do you draw the line at **[unintelligible 00:43:07]**?

Frank Carter: Because its written in scripture.

Female speaker 2: So, the fact that he found it outside of scripture?

Frank Carter: I'm not talking about him now, you asked me how do you determine whether a thing is true especially when it has to do with the Christian religion. I say that you determine whether it is true or not by whether it is in scripture. That's the reason I waited three and a half years before I started to say anything because my first thought when I saw Neville's body and I mean when I saw his body literally on the floor and it was the first corpse I'd ever seen. I knew that I had seen scripture made history but my thought was how will I ever prove this and then the thought of getting up on the platform and telling that

117

story and what I believe it to mean I broke out in a cold sweat.

Then in the course of that three years through dreams through writings I discovered that this secret story is buried there in scripture and this is the proof that its true, his credentials were sealed in scripture before he came in to the world and then he appeared he gave his message he left and then his credentials were discovered. Usually an ambassador presents his credentials first, but this ambassador gave his credentials at the last after he had departed.

[00:45:16] [END OF AUDIO]

Frank Carter Lecture 8: Dated 11/21/76

Frank Carter: I discussed the fact that traditional Christianity had taken allegory which was out of the ancient mystery schools and turned it into history. These texts were thousands of years old before even the beginning of Christianity, the religion was Egyptian. Then the Egyptian allegories were recast into Greek when the Septuagint translation of the Old Testament was made, that was the translation into Greek. So the allegory had to be recast in Greek, then one more time the allegory had to be recast into Latin. I told you that when Martin Luther reached the point of no return with the Roman Catholic church, the time when he nailed his 95 theses on the church door, shortly after that he made a translation into German. He had to invent a whole new vocabulary to take care of these word pictures describing the allegory. I also mentioned that at that point even though he had broken with the church and the pope at that time, Pope Leo 10th, had said, "What profit had not this fable of Christ brought us?", that word profit means gain. The church at that point was selling forgiveness of sins, they were making a killing. The point of this is that Luther was still under the influence of the myth, because he did not expose the myth. His doctrine was what he discovered from Paul, that you are justified by faith. That you can't do anything in this world to win grace or win salvation.

So we have the traditional Christian religion based on these ancient allegories that turned into myth. Modern scholars are agreed that if the character Paul had not grafted onto the Christian story, which is found in the gospels, the substance of the teaching of the mystery schools, that Christianity would not have survived for one generation. It would have died out almost immediately. In the letters of Paul, you have the exposition of the mystery of Christ, but Paul does not really tell you what that mystery is, he simply talks about it. It's much like hearing someone discuss a complicated mathematical theory. You're hearing everything that's said, but if mathematics is not a language for you, it might as well be in a foreign tongue. You have heard it, but you have not gotten the message.

Another point that was missed in the recasting of these allegories is that much of it was in the form of puns. Even a little child can understand a pun. You see their faces light up when the word sun is used both for son and the orbit in the sky. They suddenly understand that it's the same sound but a different meaning. Paul actually expounded the mystery in his letters, but it's all between the lines. Who is Paul? Paul reveals to you first that he is nbl. The word nbl in Hebrew means skin bag and it also means fool and it also means musical instrument. It's a very rich word, it has several meanings. In another place he reveals that he is Asar, the Egyptian god of the dead who rose from the dead, who was resurrected from the dead. This was the ancient Egyptian religion, the religion of resurrection. Paul is telling you that he had this experience, because the word asar in Hebrew, also a form of it is prisoner. In another place Paul says, "I, Paul, a prisoner of Jesus Christ". So that word means both prisoner and Asar, the bound one. I explained that the mummy is the symbol of the body in this mystery religion, because the body is the coffin of the soul. Think of it, I'm a prisoner here in this world. I'm a prisoner of this body, this nbl. The man who revealed the mystery to us has the same name as the body itself.

In the rituals in the Egyptian mystery schools the letters K, R, S, T were inscribed on the mummy case. That word is pronounced krst. You can hear that is practically like Christ. The Greek word Christ came from this Egyptian word, that's where the mystery of Christ comes from, from the ancient Egyptian mystery schools. Paul is expounding this mystery, and he's also telling you that it is a parable. It's more literally true for the imagination than it could have been, even if it had been history. Whether something is a historical fact or not, if it doesn't register in your imagination you can't comprehend it, you haven't grasped it. It really doesn't matter whether it was history or not.

120

Consider the way the Bible ends. It ends with the supplication, "Even so come Lord Jesus". Now we're the readers, we have a complete book, the Bible. We come to the end of the book, we've come to the end of the story and we wonder what happened. Did he come? The church has been waiting 2000 years. You hear the fundamentalists nowadays talking about he's coming any moment, and they're going to shake his hand, as Neville used to say. He's coming in the skies, I can hear it now. He's over Kansas now, now he's over Utah. We are the readers and we also have the vantage point in history, because we're reading the book 2000 years afterwards. Did he come?

Listen to these words of Joseph in the book of Genesis in the Old Testament, the book of Genesis, the 50th chapter. He is about to die and he says to his brothers, "God will surely visit you and deliver you out of this place". He was talking about Egypt. Remember this is a parable, this story came out of Egypt itself, and he's telling you God will surely visit you in this place and deliver you. In Deuteronomy, the 18th chapter, the 15th verse Moses makes this statement, "God will raise up from your midst a prophet like unto me. Him ye shall harken to in all things". Moses is telling by that statement that he himself is an allegory, because he says that a prophet like him is going to be raised up.

Let's look at the story of the children of Israel in Egypt. You know that they got into Egypt because there was a famine in the land. A famine can be two things. It can be an actual hunger for bread and water, or it can be the hunger for hearing the word of God. They went down into Egypt where there was food. Joseph, their brother, had gone before. They had sold him into slavery, he was a prisoner in Egypt. He rose to become second only to Pharaoh in the land, because he didn't forget the Lord God as his father. We know that principle is imagining creates reality. You see what a parable this is, he knew the secret of who the Lord really is, I am, so he rose in the land of Egypt. He did this because he had the ability to interpret dreams. You'll recall

121

that Pharaoh had the dream, the double dream, and when he interpreted the dream to Pharaoh he said because the dream was doubled it is set of God and it will shortly be brought to pass. He explained to Pharaoh all of this about the coming famine and the necessity for laying up provisions.

Years passed and that pharaoh was gone and the children of their children of their children were in bondage in Egypt and Moses, you know the story of Moses, he was saved from the slaying of all the male children by the wit of his mother in putting him in a little bull rush arc which floated on the water. The word Moses is an Egyptian word which means to draw out. Moses was raised in the palace of Pharaoh himself. We're told in the book of Acts when Steven is speaking that Moses knew all the wisdom of the Egyptians. So if Moses knew all the wisdom of the Egyptians, he knew the allegory of the mystery schools. He understood these mysteries. Moses realized that he was one of the children of Israel, and he was commanded by God to lead them out. When he was leading them out, they went out into the wilderness. To show what a parable this is, a little while back I said, "Did he come? God will surely visit you in this place and deliver you. Did he do it?" Where is he? In this world we have the story of a god who delivers his people in a book. That's where you know that story, because it's in the book. If he came, he would have to come from off of the page. That's exactly what happened, but only the imagination can understand it, because you are the most high, you are the human imagination.

In the wilderness, they're hungry and through Moses the manna is provided for them. That word manna means what is it. When they saw the manna on the ground they said, "Ma?" which is the Hebrew word for what. Then it was changed to man, which sounds like man. The manna was described as being white like a coriander seed. Remember this is a parable, and this came off of the page. The only way you can understand it is in terms of word and word plays. The word coriander comes from a word gawdad. You can hear that this is a play

122

on Neville's last name. His name was Goddard, but the English don't say Goddard, they say Goddard. The coriander is described as being white. The word for white in Hebrew is lavan, and lavan spelled backwards is naval, which again is a play on Neville. Here in this description of the manna which fed them, this was spiritual food because Paul makes it very clear in First Corinthians the 10th chapter that they were fed with spiritual food. On this level you have the book, you can see the book it's in space, it's in time, but you open it up and you read it and then you're in eternity, because only the mind can read the marks on the page. The story exists in heaven, and heaven is up here in your own human imagination.

In this same 10th chapter of First Corinthians Paul says this, "I would not have you ignorant of the fact that our fathers were under the clouds and in the sea and were baptized unto Moses in the clouds and in the sea". In the images of the mystery school, baptism was the allegory for the descent into matter, because you know that your body is over 90% water. So when you, the one I am, came down into this experience, you were baptized into the sea of matter. This is another way of setting forth the incarnation. Just in case that wouldn't be enough to show mystery, there's a double clue in this statement. The word for cloud in the Greek language is nephele. That shouldn't give anyone any trouble because in English, we don't say I have to go, we say I have to go. The V converts to the F sound. Here you have nephele, so Paul is telling you that our fathers were under the cloud. Here's a double pun, under the cloud of flesh and also under the cloud Neville, who revealed this mystery to you. You're elect, you believed him, you went to his lectures, you heard what he had to say. You didn't have one shred of proof, but you believed it. Our fathers were baptized unto Moses, Moses is the one who draws himself out so he is the resurrected man. Neville told that when he awoke in his skull, he drew himself out of his own skull just as a child is born from the womb of a woman. So we have nephele, the cloud, and you remember in another place God appeared in the form of a cloud. The statement is all over that book of Exodus. Abraham is our father, it actually means father of a multitude. Paul is telling you that our fathers had this experience, which is really a way in a parable form of telling that he's not talking about history, he's talking to the people who understand what is being said, the brothers who went before. This is the story of the brothers who came down.

A lady at my second lecture had a vision while I was speaking. She's not here today, but she very graciously allowed me to tell what happened. She said that I had been speaking about five minutes when she saw a light silhouette my form, it wasn't just the head but the whole form. She blinked, she thought perhaps her eyes were playing tricks on her. She closed her eyes and when she opened them again she said the light was much brighter. She was fighting it, she didn't want it to take place. Then she could see that the light was trying to form itself into some image. I don't understand whether at this point the image blocked the view of me or whether the image went over to the side. It went over to the side and when it went over to the side, it formed into what looked like Abraham Lincoln as he is seen in the Lincoln memorial in Washington. I saw it last night on TV, a view of the Lincoln memorial. She looked closer and she saw that it wasn't Abraham Lincoln, it was Neville. Then it drifted off toward the wall. She said she got goose pimply and wanted to tell her friend sitting next to her but she realized that she couldn't, so she settled back down to concentrate. Then she said the whole thing began all over again and she said to herself, "What the heck is going on here?" She fought it this time, she tried to keep it from happening. The whole thing repeated just as it had the first time.

I love this, she said, "Why me?", meaning her. Why did she have the experience? I love that, because that's exactly what I'm saying, "Why me?" I don't understand. Then she said because of what happened and how it happened she felt that this is an adumbration of some kind and she would like me to make some comment on it. I feel very definitely that it is an adumbration for her and for this work. To me it means that the depth of her being had projected this eternal truth, which was written before the world was and it's sealed in everyone in this world. That's another parable of the book. The book in time and space is a parable of the book that is sealed within you, because then you are the book, you wrote it. So the depth of her being projected this truth, and what I loved about this is that I had a very hard time deciding whether to interpret the parable of nbl the fool the way I did. I thought perhaps I could be mistaken, perhaps I was taking too many liberties, but I was finally forced to make that interpretation because of the pun play in the Hebrew language. I had no choice, so I decided I have to tell it. I don't mind telling you from the time I had begun these lectures I haven't been all that secure because how do I know, really. I don't have these kind of visions. Here while I was talking at that second lecture about Neville, nbl the fool, the covering, the body, she had the vision of Neville sitting as Abraham Lincoln and Abraham Lincoln is the great emancipator.

Moses was the great emancipator because he got the children of Israel, and this is a spiritual story, he got them out of the Earth experience toward the promised land, which is the promise of being born from above.

Another interesting thing is that I have had two dreams of the brothers, widely spaced. In one in I was in a hospital, which is natural for me because in my work I go into hospitals and doctor's offices all day. There I was in a hospital and then it was as if I awoke and I looked and I saw these big brothers, and I knew that they were the brothers. They said, "We know that you're having a hard time here, but we're with you. You are our dear little brother, and we're looking over you". That was one vision. Another time in vision I looked up at the sky and here was rank up on rank of clouds in the form of Abraham Lincoln. So you see, we're all one. Her vision was tuned in with my vision of the brothers because here they were, the brothers were all alike, all Abraham Lincoln. Abraham is the father, the father of the multitude, and that is the promise, that we will awaken as God the father. Needless to say, I was thrilled to death that she had this vision, because don't forget that the cloud is nephele. When Paul is quoting the Old Testament, he is almost always quoting the Septuagint, which is the Greek translation. When he says cloud, he's saying the word nephele. You can hear that this in some way probably came from an identical source or maybe actually out of the Hebrew itself, because the Greek language is not as old as the Hebrew language.

Narrator: This was a lecture by Frank Carter given on November, 21st 1976. It ends here. Run the tape fast forward to the end of the tape, then turn over to hear the next lecture.

[00:30:33] [END OF AUDIO]

Frank Carter Lecture 9: Dated 11/28/76

Frank Carter: She told me that she felt that it was an adumbration and she wanted me to comment on it. She had the vision not once but twice. The reason I was so thrilled about her having this vision is that the depth of her soul, of her being was projecting into the screen of space this eternal vision which I was talking about at that very moment. As I told you, when I began this work I really couldn't be sure whether I was interpreting right or not. Here, while I was speaking, the depth of her being had this vision. The vision was of Neville. This was especially uplifting to me, because my message is about a man named Neville who was in history. After he departed it became clear that this man who revealed the secret to us of the promise, that is that David is your eternal son, this man who revealed that secret in history has his name concealed in scripture itself.

The name Neville occurs in pun form in the Hebrew language as the word nbl. Nbl in Hebrew means skin bag, which is our condition, we're skin bags. When you look at the human body, you are looking at the means by which I am in the world. You know that this was Neville's teaching, that there is only one being in the world. His name is I Am Forever, that is your eternal nature, but while you are here you are wearing these garments of skin. The name for that garment, the hidden name for it is nbl, and that was his name.

Last week I spoke about the book which is both in time and space and the book which is you. Think of it this way, the Bible is God's novel. Hear how close to Neville the word novel is. You could even go farther and say that the Bible is Neville's novel. The author wrote this story. Paul, for all intents and purposes, was the founder of the Christian religion. If he had not grafted onto the Christian movement the substance of the mystery school, that religion would not have lasted one generation it would have died out. There is no record of Paul in the

127

ancient world. The only way that we know Paul is that we read his words on the page. Only the most high can read the words, and that's you. When you look at the marks on the page you read the words, the images form in your mind, and then you're in eternity. The mind is eternity itself, the human imagination is eternity, yet eternity is contained in this book. Paul is the one who explains all of the mysteries. He doesn't actually explain them, he expounds them. Who is Paul? They admit that they don't know what the name Paul means. Paul in Hebrew means maker, your maker is your husband. It's also actually the name of a portion of the Hebrew verb itself. So here is Paul, the maker, who is explaining, expounding these mysteries of Christ and the religion.

Last week I told about Moses leading the children of Israel out of Egypt. You know that Egypt is your own body. While Moses was leading them out, God appeared to them in the form of a cloud. When Paul is writing these words, he is writing in the Greek tongue. When he tells you that God appeared in the form of a cloud, he is saying God appeared in the form nephele. You can hear that this again is a play on the name Neville. In English we don't say I have to go, we say I have to go, you have the V converting to the F sound. Elsewhere at the very beginning of Acts when the central character called Jesus is ascending into heaven, his disciples are standing watching the ascension. Then we're told a cloud received him from their sight. Immediately there appeared two men beside them and they said, "Why stand ye gazing into heaven? This same Jesus will come in like manner as ye have seen him go". How did he go? A cloud received him from their sight.

In the book of Revelation at the very beginning of the 10th chapter we are told, "An angel came down from heaven clothed with a cloud". You know that an angel is a messenger. A messenger has come in the function of an ambassador to deliver a message. So this angel comes down clothed as a nephele, delivers his message, and this angel has a book in his hands. He tells the one having the vision to take the book and eat it, that it will be like honey in his mouth, but it will be bitter in his belly. Elsewhere in the Old Testament we're told to eat the book. Of course on this literal level that would be sheer nonsense, so obviously the message is spiritual.

In the wilderness when Moses was leading the children out, the manna appeared, and they fed on the manna. Paul told us that this manna was spiritual food, in other words it was the word of God. That was Neville's theme, he was always preaching the word of God. Now listen to the description of the manna, remember this is a parable. The story never took place on Earth, but it takes place in eternity when you read the words and when you gather the clues which put everything in place. The manna is described as being like a coriander seed and white. The word coriander in the Hebrew language is God. It's spelled G-A-D, but it's pronounced God, so here is a play on our English word God. That word, gad, which means coriander comes from the Hebrew word gaddad. Neville's last name was Goddard, but the English don't say Goddard, they say Goddard. Here concealed in the words themselves is the name of the man who came into history and delivered this message. As if that weren't enough, the coriander seed is described as being white. The word for white in Hebrew is levan and levan read backwards or in our custom of reading from right to left is navel. So here in the description of the manna are the first and last names of this man who came into history. His message was it's all about you. It's a parable, you wrote the book. You are the elohim here in these garments of flesh, in these nbls. You're actually called after his name.

As I said the name Paul itself means maker which shows that the maker, the most high, wrote the story. He tells you other things about himself, in one place he says, "I have become a fool". The word for fool is nbl, so he's telling you he became Neville. In another place he says, "I, Paul, a prisoner of Jesus Christ". That word, prisoner, in Hebrew is asir, and that comes from the Hebrew word asar. Asar is the ancient Egyptian god of the dead. As I told you earlier in the lecture, Paul took the ancient secret teachings of the mystery school, these

129

teachings were thousands of years old. Took these teachings and buried them in his letters so that it could not be seen until the one came into history to activate the story as it were. Simply a story on a page, but into history comes the man who has the experiences, and then scripture starts to come alive. Paul is telling you that he is Asar, and the story of Asar is that he was resurrected from the dead, and this is Neville's great message that he was resurrected from the dead by seeing his son, David.

There were two captivities. The one captivity was in Egypt. There's no record that the Hebrew people were ever there. Nevertheless, we're told that they came out of Egypt, they were led by this man, Moses, they had that experience of being fed by the manna which is our experience, it's a parable for us. There's no record of that captivity. There is another captivity of the Hebrew people, it is known as the Babylonian captivity. They were actually carried away to Babylon and there they remained until Cyrus, the king of Persia, decreed that the people should be released and go back to Jerusalem and build the temple. I'm not talking about history now, this is a parable, because that's your condition, that's my condition. The one captivity is the captivity of the body to be a prisoner here in this body. The other captivity is the Babylonian captivity, which is to be a prisoner of confusion, because babble in Hebrew means confusion. All you have to do is look around at the world today and you see mass confusion. If ever there was a need to be delivered out of a captivity, out of confusion, it's today.

When the children of Israel are freed to leave Babylon and go back to Jerusalem, their leader is Ezra. Ezra comes from the Hebrew word azar. Everywhere you look in scripture this mystery of asar, the ancient god of the dead, the ancient story of the mystery schools is buried. Azar is their leader. On the way there is much talk about taking treasure to the temple. The word for treasure in Hebrew it otzar. You hear another play on Asar. When they get to Jerusalem the construction of the temple is begun and the people gather, this is the part I love because it's our tale, the people gather before the water gate. There can't be anyone here who hasn't heard about Watergate. In a parable, here are the people in time and space before the water gate. In other words an event which is very prominent in our world. They gather before the water gate and Ezra, who is really Asar, the one who has risen from the dead, Ezra reads to them from the book and reveals the meaning of the book.

You see how literally true this is for the human imagination, because this is exactly what happened in our experience with Neville. He came, he told us that he had been resurrected from the dead. Before that, he taught imagining creates reality for years, showing that the human imagination is really the most high. You can have anything in this world you want, simply imagine it. Then he had his experience with the promise and he began telling that, because he felt this was a message he had really been sent to deliver. When Ezra is reading to the people out of the book he gives the understanding to the word, so that they understand the meaning of the book. Then they remember the law of Moses, and they understand how to interpret that.

Paul, as I said before, reveals that he is both nbl, the fool, the skin bag, and that he is Asar, the one who fulfills this ancient mystery religion of being resurrected. His message he consistently called the gospel of Christ. He was the first one to use the word gospel. It's a little confusing because in the Bible in the New Testament, first you have the four gospels, then you have the book of Acts, then you have these series of letter written supposedly to the churches. They're written to you, the reader, giving you information about this mystery. That word, gospel, was taken from the Hebrew term good news, because they were announcing the good news of Christ. That mystery was hidden from the ages until Neville came into the world and revealed it. That gospel of Christ is that you are the eternal father and that when you see your eternal son David you have awakened from this dream, from this world of the wheel, and you're ready to go back to eternity. That word,

131

gospel, is taken from the Hebrew word basar. You can hear another play on Asar, but this time there's a B in front of it. What makes it conclusive is that this word has two meanings. It means both good news and it means flesh. Here we come right back to the core of the mystery, the word made flesh, and this Hebrew word basar means flesh, and that is the gospel.

In one of his lectures the last year, Neville told that Cyrus is actually David. It threw me at the time, but he did make that statement that this king Cyrus is David, because in Isaiah in the 45th chapter we have these words by the Lord, "Cyrus is my shepherd". Then, "Thus sayeth the Lord to Cyrus, his anointed". You know that the qualifier for the messiah, for the Christ, is to have been anointed, and David was the anointed one, the messiah. Here again in a parable, this release from captivity in Babylon was activated by Cyrus, by the anointed. You can't get out of Babylon until you see your son David. It's all about you yet concealed as a mystery.

Allow me to share an experience I had in 1973, late summer or early fall. One night I was winding a clock, my mother gave it to me it's an antique clock, I thought I was being very careful. As I wound it, the spring gave way and it stopped on the hour 10:00. That night in vision, in dream, Neville appeared to me lecturing. I was in a group like this, I was in the audience. He said, "Ten, and now you must jump. Ten, and now Bethany, and now you must jump". He did this over and over. When I got up in the morning I went to the concordance, which I use. He told us very definitely in his lectures that you cannot understand scripture if you don't use a concordance. You must use it to find out what these words mean. I looked up 10, and at that point I had not heard of the story of the ancient mystery school of about Osiris or, as he's known in Egyptian, Asar. I looked up Bethany, but I didn't get anywhere there, because it's defined as meaning house of days. Death means house and the word for days. I didn't get anywhere there, because the word date does not appear in scripture. The only time they used the word date in the concordance was to define this word, but the word date itself does not appear in scripture.

Then just a few days later I was talking with a friend and she happened to mention some books and mentioned the Egyptian mythology and what have you. I said, "Something tells me that I must read these books".She said, "Fine", so she lent them to me. Almost immediately when I opened the book I discovered the story of the raising of Lazarus, which appears in the gospel of John. Here again in scripture itself is a concealed form of the ancient story of the mystery schools. In the story Asar is lying in mummy form in a cave, and his son Horus goes to the mouth of the cave and calls to him and says, "El Asar come forth". El Asar rose from the dead and came forth. In the course of time, El Asar took the form Elasarus and then finally became Lazarus, who was the one raised by the character Jesus in that gospel.

On the mummy case, in the reenactment of this ancient mystery, were inscribed the letters K, R, S, T. That is where the word Christ comes from, from the ancient Egyptian ritual of resurrection. Then it passed into the Greek tongue, so when Paul is talking about the mystery of Christ and the gospel of Christ, he was undoubtedly a member of the mystery schools and he understood these mysteries. When he said, "The gospel of Christ", he was saying the basar, which is a play on Asar of Christ. Basar means flesh, that's what those four letters meant in Egyptian, the fleshed one, the one who is in flesh. As I've said before, this sounds like a ridiculous story, outrageous, but you have to remember that this is the terminology of the mind that built the great pyramid, an astonishing mind. This was their way of taking the mystery of the incarnation and presenting it in a vivid form so that it would make an indelible impression on the mind.

Just summing up, we have the word nephele which means cloud, which is also a play on the name of a man who revealed this mystery to us. If he hadn't come and told his story, none of us would be here today, we wouldn't have found it out by ourselves. This was another mystery of scripture that scripture would be made literally true as an experience for the human imagination. You are the cloud too. Robert Blake in his poem *Little Boy Lost* speaks of the cloud of flesh. That's we, a cloud of flesh here in this world. Think of it this way too, in this world there is nothing which is such a perfect image for the imagination as the clouds. The cloud can assume any form, and it's a perfect exercise for the imagination to watch these big, puffy clouds on marvelous summer days and see the shapes, the animals, the people. Perfect exercise for the imagination. Here is the word cloud containing his name and our nature.

Then we have the word nbl which is skin bag, which is the body. Again his name describing our nature. The the word asar which also in Hebrew means to bind. You know that the mummy is bound, the mummy is the symbol of the body in this world, because the body is the coffin of the soul. You couldn't possibly forget the imagery there. Then in the Old Testament there is a musical instrument, which is called the naval asar. These two words were joined together, again hiding the mystery. They believe it's a musical instrument, but it's also a means of concealing the ancient religion, which was the religion of Asar and Neville, the man who came into the world and fulfilled it.

I've told you before that the man who saved Roman Catholicism, even though it was completely on a false premise, was Saint Augustine. He formulated a workable theology, and it was he who formulated the trinity. This man said this, "That which is known as the Christian religion existed among the ancients and never did not exist from the very beginning of the human race.

The day after I gave my first lecture in June, a friend of mine sent me a clipping from the Los Angeles times for that day. In it was the most fascinating story about an archaeological excavation in Sierra of a kingdom called Ebla. From these excavations they have determined

134

from 15,000 clay tablets that all of this story contained in the Old Testament was known to these people, because they found the names Jerusalem, David, Abraham, right down the line. The interesting thing is that according to the dates this means that 1000 years before it's reckoned was Jerusalem. They have to date back 1000 years before. This is showing that these scriptures existed in the ancient world. As a matter of fact, 3500 years before this supposed event took place, these scriptures were already venerable with age in Egypt. They were simply copied and handed down. Then you might say that the demand created the supply. Here's a town written about, alright, we'll make a town. So, they took this and appropriated it and made history out of it. The land Sierra itself is a form of Asur. You can hear again Asar. This name, Asur, came from the Acadian word asaru. Even the land of Egypt, the modern day name for the land of Egypt is derived from this word asaru, and it means basically to encompass, to hedge around. Which again comes back to the body, because we are hedged in. Here is the land of Sierra itself, asur, a play on Asar.

This is incredible, there is a recently published book called *The Thirteenth Tribe* by Arthur Koestler, this is history. The man makes the point that the Jews in eastern Europe did not actually come from Palestine, so they are not Semitic. They actually came from a nation called Khazar. There was actually a kingdom named Khazar. Here again in history as a kind of joke you might say, the author had a nation adopt the Jewish religion. They did this because they were right in the middle between the Christian empire and Islam. They didn't want to go either way, so they decided to adopt Judaism, and they adopted it in all of its particulars; the Hebrew language, the law, everything which set the advocates of the Jewish religion apart. The name of this nation was Khazar. All you have to do is take away the KH and you have azar. He believes that this is where the Jews in eastern Europe came from, that they are actually Turkish. Here we have the parable, thousands of years old, which was not history. Then we have what was considered to be history, and then after that the religion was preserved by a country which coincidentally had this name, and in the Hebrew language itself you have multitudes of word plays on this name, Asar. Now, are there any questions?

Audience Member 1: I think my basic question has to do with the fact that if I understand your speech and Neville's remarks also about this is a standing order, this resurrection, it goes back where you're talking about Osiris. In other words resurrection is an eternal drama. What is the significance then of the duality between the prophecies of the Old Testament and the fulfillment of the New Testament in time? What happened since the day of John the Baptist that wasn't happening before that?

Frank: Good question. If I recall, Neville said that in history there have undoubtedly been those who had the experience, but they were not commissioned to tell it, so they concealed it in the form of allegory. So, the story could be preserved, but at the same time it was hidden.

Audience Member 1: So, it was happening in man, in individuals?

Frank: Yes, I believe he said that. I have no authority for making a statement on that, but I believe that he did say that.

Audience Member 1: That's one side. The other side is that as it says in Daniel, I don't understand it, I don't know what it's all about because it hasn't been fulfilled yet. Then at the time of the New Testament, the day of John the Baptist, at some point and time and place in history, this happened. If it had been erupting, what happened that was new at that point in history?

Frank: You mean at the supposed time that it took place?

Audience Member 1: Yes, at the supposed time in the New Testament 2000 years ago.

Frank: Apparently these ancient writings were released to the public at large and it was misinterpreted. That was the point at which it was turned into history. You have the fundamentalists nowadays who believe that this character Jesus actually was in Palestine 2000 years ago, and he had the experiences which are recorded in the gospels. Studies in comparative religion have shown that this story, as I said before, was 3500 years old. It was lifted out of the Egyptian texts, and it's really the story of Horus. There are 180 points of similarity between Horus and the character Jesus.

These texts were lifted out and the public got a hold of them, and you might say that the demand created the supply. They wanted it to be history. There was a struggle in the early church, which boils down to the controversy over whether scripture should be interpreted as allegory or history. The history side won, but it was only the writings of Paul that saved the religion, because he grafted on to this corpus of literature his secret doctrine of the mystery schools. There can be no doubt that he understood the mystery of Christ's resurrection, but it's all between the lines.

Audience Member 1: There's another quote about resurrection that says since the day of John the Baptist, the kingdom has been taken violently. Violent men take it violently. In other words, something new started happening around that time that wasn't happening before in the mystery schools.

Frank: That could be, yes.

Audience Member 1: The mystery schools were anesthetized in a way. An out of body experience would have been experienced. Since that time, they have been experiencing an in body – that's the way I read it, that's my question right now. What is it that took place in the time of Jesus Christ that hadn't happened before?

Frank: Harry?

Harry: Neville on numerous talks, one in particular that I would call these are the prophets and visions. The reason that it is written, they wrote their own visions in this allegorical form here, and all these things had been taking place all during that time, it had just never been brought out to where the everyday person could understand it.

Audience Member 1: The point he made in one lecture, he said Daniel said I've written it, I don't understand it, I haven't the slightest idea what it's about. Close the book and wait.

Harry: The other question that you were asking, if I recall right, Neville also stated when the promise starts taking place in you, it comes with violent action. In other words it storms you, it overtakes you, it's like an earthquake. In fact one of them is called the three inner earthquakes that take place within you but actually just about tear you up.

Audience Member 1: In other words, at a point in history something changed in the character of this resurrection.

Frank: Undoubtedly.

Audience Member 1: In other words, 2000 years before the time of Paul, this was coming in a different form than it is since then.

Frank: I see all this as a parable for the most high, and that's you.

[00:45:20] [END OF AUDIO]

Frank Carter Lecture 10: Dated 12/05/76

Male speaker: December the 5th 1976. A lecture by Frank Carter.

Frank Carter: The continuing theme of these talks has been scripture Neville and you. Now in the course of the preceding five lectures I have attempted to show that that book which we call the Bible was never history, that was Neville's message. He came in to our world in to history. First, he taught the law then he had the experience which he called The Promise.

The Promise was his experience of being born from above out of his own skull. Then some time later he had another experience in which he saw his son David the eternal son David and that is when he realized he had awakened as God the Father. Now as Paul said in one place, "We have the babes in Christ" that is to say the little ones and understanding who are still feeding on milk. Then comes the time as they grow up they are ready for stronger meant and this is what Neville delivered. He delivered the strong meat of the meaning of this book we call the Bible.

Now the Apostle Paul for all intents and purposes founded the Christian religion. Scholars are agreed that if he had not grafted on to the corpus of this story his message about the Gospel of Christ that that religion could not have survived one generation. Then I showed that Paul identified himself as Neville because he said in one place, "I have become a fool in glorying" now the word for fool in the Hebrew language is Neville, Nabal. So, Paul is telling you that he became Neville this man because Neville had all of Paul's experiences. Paul had the experience of being resurrected from the dead. He doesn't tell it outright, it's between the lines.

Now what I have to tell today is very very difficult, you might say it's a bombshell. Yesterday when I was thinking about what I would say today I had many misgivings because what I want to talk about today is so easily misunderstood it is so easily ridiculed that one must be very careful.

Well I went to sleep night last night with this on my mind and I woke up in the middle of the night and I didn't feel any better about it, but I went back to sleep and while I was sleeping I had a dream a vision. I had a ghost story. I thought this was funny because I began my series of lectures this year on Halloween. In this ghost story I was in a corridor of a large building and I saw a ghost and I was scared nearly out of my wits and I ran in to the room where I was to speak and I told the people waiting for me, I said, "I just saw a ghost" and before I could saw anything more their mouths all dropped open and they had a wide-eyed look and I realized that the ghost had appeared in the door behind me and they were seeing what I saw.

I turned around, when I turned around it was too late he was gone. Well I followed him through those doors trying to catch him and then I became frightened again so I said, "Better leave well enough alone". Now the point of all this is that the depths of my being was giving me a message that if you tell what you have seen, what you have experience, then there is every possibility that others will understand what you are talking about. So, I proceed now.

I want to talk today about the Holy Ghost, the Holy Spirit. You know that the early church according to the story as its recording in the Book of Acts caught fire because they had the experience of the Holy Spirit. The Apostles were the ones who had the ability to confer this gift by the laying on of hands. I've often heard orthodox churchmen say that if there had been no day of Pentecost, that is the day when the spirit came down as cloven tongues of fire to the people who were assembled. That is that event had never happened the church would of have to have invented it to explain the fervor the zeal with which the early church began to move forward.

140

Now we know that all of that is a parable, that has been my theme these past five lectures. That everything written in scripture is a parable of what is written within you because you are the book, you wrote the book. When I first realized what had happened after I found Neville's body I actually saw Neville's corpse and at this time I think it's appropriate to tell you that the word for corpse in Hebrew is another form of the name Neville. It's absolutely astonishing how his name appears in the Hebrew and in the Greek because he was the one through whom this story was to be revealed.

When I realized what had happened I went in to a state of virtual shock because I knew in my own mind that I had seen that written word made history. That everything that had been a parable an allegory before had been made actual history in our world and then I discovered that it was concealed in scripture in the form of puns in the Hebrew and the Greek languages.

Now when I found these things I was terribly disturbed because I couldn't tell them to anyone. In the first place, I knew what they would think and the next place certain followers of Neville felt that I had betrayed him by the interpretation I was giving to these findings, but the greatest worry of all was that I could not talk to Mrs. Goddard, she was terribly ill. She didn't even know what had happened.

There were times when I felt perhaps I could broach the subject, I could tell her what happened and what it had revealed, but then I could see that her health was too frail to take the chance of another shock.

In 1974 in March one day she said to me, and this was not characteristic of her, she said, "What's going on?" and a million thoughts went through my head I thought, "Good heavens has someone told her a garbled version?" I said, "What do you mean?" She said, "Neville" at this point she was writing, she had lost the ability to speak. Her recovery was a miracle because she had 22 operations in two years and you know what a shock to the system one operation is, but she wrote, "Neville" and I said, "What do you mean?" and she said, "Do you know anything?" and I said, "Well yes I do, I think I know all about it" and I thought perhaps it was a passing whim so I didnt write her a letter as I had promised her.

Then the next time she saw me she wrote me a furious note especially the extravagant movements and she said, "Where is my letter?" I said, "Oh very well alright you want your letter" So I was forced to sit down and formulate what I had experienced what I understood and put it on paper. Now the gist of what I wrote her is this. That because he died as Judas as it is recorded in scripture this is the key that opens the door. This is the point of departure towards the understanding of the other mysteries because when I began to move forward from this experience of seeing his corpse, the corpse of the man who claimed to have awakened as God the Father in this world. Now that is a wild statement.

Nevertheless, week after week from the public platform he said "I am not speculating I am not theorizing I have awakened as God the Father and the same experience is in store for you".

As I began to move forward with this key especially his last note, he wrote, "This is my true experience of the last supper. Judas betrayed the Messianic secret". Now Judas died by falling headlong and he burst asunder in the midst and all his bowels gushed out. Now this is the way Neville died, he shed every drop of blood in his body and the corpse I saw was exactly what I saw in my dream, in my vision.

Now moving forward, you find many many cryptic remarks by Paul, for instance in Philippians he's talking about the Gospel and you know that was Paul's words about the Gospel and I explained last week that word gospel connects directly what we call in the Christian religion with the most ancient religion in the world which was the religion of resurrection, Egyptian religion of resurrection. In this first chapter of Philippians Paul says this, "I want you to know that the things which

142

happened unto me have fallen out for the furtherance of the Gospel" and just before that he had made a reference to the bowels.

So, you see all of these clues are concealed until the man comes in to the world who is going to activate all of this.

So, I went on to explain some of these things in my letter to Mrs. Goddard and I ended it by saying, "I understand because Neville had all of the experiences of Paul. That he is the image of Paul" and in another place Paul tells again in a cryptic way that he is the image of the Holy Spirit. Now I dared to write her this and then I told her that his name in Greek means cloud and that an angel came down from heaven clothed with a cloud. In other words, a Nephele a Neville came down from heaven and he had a book in his hand. So, I ended her the letter by showing her that his name appears and reveals that he was the destined historic one to reveal this mystery.

Well I didn't hear anything from her she didn't say yay or nay. Then almost a year later as a throwaway one day in conversation she said, "Oh by the way, when I fused with Neville last February" and I thought, "When you fused with Neville" because you know that was Neville's great experience in the beginning, he fused with infinite love back in 1929 and then he was instructed to go out and his instructions were down with the blue bloods and he told us that term blue bloods did not mean anything in this world pertaining to society, a person's station in society, it meant church protocol established orthodoxy. In other words, the institution which had completely garbled the message, misinterpreted it.

Well I couldn't get anything out of her because I didn't have the nerve to ask her to tell me her experience because obviously it was a very personal glorious experience and you simply don't talk about it, but she did tell me that she fused with Neville. Now the reason I am telling all of this is that even before Neville departed there were people who had the experience in the spirit of Neville as the heavenly bridegroom and I think most of you have heard this at one time or another.

It was a subject which he did not like to talk about because as I said when I began my words today it is so easily misunderstood and it is so easily ridiculed, but nevertheless we have in scripture your maker is your husband. Now the word maker in Hebrew is Paul. So here again Paul is your husband and Neville is Paul because he had Paul's experiences and told him and his credentials about these experiences are sealed in scripture.

So, she experienced him as the heavenly bridegroom. Now as I'm saying so often all of this is a parable because you are the infinite being, you are the only being there ever was there ever will be, nevertheless you consented to come down in to this world of the prison. You consented to come down in to this world of confusion which is Babylon and you are a prisoner here. Now you came in to this world through an act of lovemaking, that's the way our bodies are created through acts of love, and you are going to depart this world of Egypt the body and this world of Babylon the confusion of the mind through another act of lovemaking and that is the function of the Holy Spirit.

Now last week I made two mistakes when I was lecturing. One was a glaring error. I tried to say William Blake and it Robert Break, Break Blake. So, an error. I tried to say that William Blake wrote in his poem Little Black Boy the mystery of the human body as the cloud of flesh and I called it Little Boy Lost, now that's more obscure.

Nevertheless this poem is Little Black Boy, that was what I tried to quote in this lovely lovely poem which I cannot quote from memory the point is made the black boy's mother tells him that he came in to this world just as the white child did to wear this could of flesh to protect him from the beams of his father in the sky, his father the sun, so that he could bear the beams just stay here a while so that he could learn to bear the beams of love because the greatest force in our world is the sun

144

and that was the ancient Egyptian symbol for our father because it's our life, take the sun away we have no life.

When I discovered I made these mistakes I started digging in to my Blake books, and this is what I love, I found what I'm going to tell you in two books which Mrs. Goddard gave me as a gift they weren't books which Neville owned, she went out and bought them as a gift for me and this is where I found what I am going to tell you. There is another place in which Blake uses the word cloud, now remember the word for cloud in Greek is Nephele a play on the name Neville and Neville told us that he had had communion with Blake, Blake knew who he was. They communed on the eternal level.

This other use of the cloud as the body is in the book of Thel T-H-E-L, I didn't have time to read it I simply took the condensed form of the story as told in this Blake dictionary. Briefly told it's the story of a virgin name Thel who lives in the land of Har H-A-R. Now Har in Blakes terminology meant self- love and she tended her flocks by the river and she was bored with her existence and then she became aware of another place she had heard of the place of death and she began asking, "Should I go there?" and she consulted the Lily of the Valley which was her own innocence and then she consulted the cloud and the cloud means the male fertilizer. Now remember the name cloud is a form of Neville, Neville the heavenly bridegroom, Neville the male fertilizer.

Now remember this is all a parable because sex on this level is merely a symbol of heavenly reunion, heavenly union. It's only a symbol of that.

She talks with the cloud then in her imagination she projects herself in to this world of death and while she is lying there in her grave in this world of death, in other words she projects herself in her imagination in to the garment which would be worn in that world which is the body and while she is lying there she hears the moans and the cries of those who are going through the furnaces who were going through all the worst experiences of the five sense and then she's terrified and so she goes immediately back.

Now you can see this is a parable of one who did not come in to the earth experience. That last day I spent with Neville I told him that I'd had this vision as it were downtown about being deep deep in the heart of woodland which is Blakes word for this world of the furness and he said, "Yes and there are those who believe that no one ever returns" and I said, "You see them?" and he said, "Yes I see them" and I said, "Well do you see those who have come out?" and he said, "Yes and they are the most glorified beings you could ever imagine".

So, he was telling me that he sees both the brothers the Elohim who have not come in and he sees those who have come out and when he told that he knew that he was about to depart, to go back to eternity as a glorified brother.

Now this story of Thel is a parable of one who did not come in because in the imagination this virgin Thel realized that she would have to fall asleep, lose her memory and have to go through all of these experiences. Now in the Book of Acts the 20th Chapter the 9th Verse is the story of a brother who came in and what happened to him? His name is Eutychus. This is really an amusing story. Paul is preaching and as the text says he preached very long and this lad Eutychus was sitting up on the third balcony and he fell asleep and when he fell asleep because of Paul's long preaching he fell off the balcony down in to the middle of the room where everyone was assembled listening to Paul.

Now with that Paul fell upon him and when he fell upon him the lad was resurrected. Now this sounds like one more miracle story, but if you look in your concordance Strong's exhaustive concordance and look up the meanings of these words then we get to the core of the meaning, the grain, you take away the husk and reveal the grain of the truth. Eutychus in Greek means fortunate. Now when Paul fell down on him that word in Greek for the verb means to seize with affection more

146

or less violently, to seize with affection.

Now I explained last week that God in Hebrew comes from Goddart which is a form of Neville's last name and this word God means coriander and that's the way the manna was described. The manna which was the spiritual food was described as coriander and that word is God which comes from the Hebrew word Goddart, because we don't say-- the English say Neville Goddart, they drop that R, so here is this word in the Hebrew tongue itself.

Now there are two other meanings for God. Gad which sounds like our word God. One is fortunate another is a Babylonian deity which I think is interesting because we are in Babylon here, we are in this world of confusion and fortune is a very great god in our world. So, you see its all parable. Now elsewhere in the Old Testament we're told that God, G-A-D, was David's seer, F-E-E-R, and that word seer F-E-E-R in Hebrew means to behold in vision. No let me go over this again God is the one who beholds David in vision. You see how this story which Neville told is concealed.

So here was Eutychus the fortunate one who fell asleep and he fell down from the third level which I'm sure have some meaning which I don't know and he was as one dead and Paul who was the maker who is Neville who is the image of the Holy Spirit seized him with affection in an act of love making, this was all in the spirit, and then the lad was resurrected. So Eutychus is David's seer. It's all concealed here in this story.

Now there is yet one more revelation which Paul has of himself. In the first Corinthians, the 4th Chapter the 14th Verse he makes this statement, "Though ye have many instructors in Christ you have only one father. Through Christ Jesus I have begotten you through the Gospel". Let me say that again, "Though you have many instructors in Christ nevertheless you have only one father, I have begotten you through the Gospel" Paul is talking about himself, he is revealing himself as the father which is not surprising as the word Paul means maker in Hebrew.

The word which is the revelation and I'm not selling anything because I heard Neville say this, but I didn't understand the full implication at the time. The full core of the meaning is contained in the word begotten. Now that word begotten in Greek means to procreate and act of love making. So here again Paul is telling you that he is the heavenly bridegroom, that he is the heavenly impregnator for the soul and the soul is a virgin.

You see here again the shadow of the heavenly, everything here on earth is the shadow of the heavenly, the real the real meaning. So the soul here is a virgin until the soul has union with the heavenly bridegroom and my part today is to identify the image of this heavenly bridegroom as the man we knew as Neville. You see this image was sealed within the depths of your being before you even came in to this world. Otherwise as Blake says you would keep falling deeper deeper falling falling, truth has limits error or not and so this is the means by which you are to depart this world. This is the means by which you are to have the promise.

In the images of the ancient mystery schools was contained this story, not what I told you about Neville, but was sold the essence of this story that the God, that's you, I am the God came down to give his higher nature to these animal beings. I'm an animal look at me, the animal nature. Nevertheless, these animals were to be raised up to the status of divinity by feeding on this higher nature and it was typified as bread. This is where Holy Communion comes from, fed on my bread.

Now the only way you can assimilate food is to grind it to pieces otherwise your body can't assimilate. So, this higher nature was ground to pieces. Neville told us that this is the story of the fragmented man, the ground up man, we came in to this world we fell as one man and fragmented.

148

This is the story of the fall. Now the word for fall in Hebrew is Nefal another play on Neville. Wherever you look in scripture its Neville's novel. He told us that the blood is the consciousness. So, you eat the bread of the higher nature and you drink the blood and Paul claimed absolute understanding of the Lords Supper.

In First Corinthians, the 11th Chapter he discusses the Lords Supper he says, "I receive this from the Lord himself" and he said, "The Lord said take this is my body which is broken for you" after supper he said, "Here take the cup this is my blood which is shed for you". The bread and the blood and the wine shed to give life to the animal nature here in this world of woodland.

After Paul tells that he says, "When I come I'll set everything in order" now my understanding of that is that I'll see that everything is straightened out and also that I will explain everything and Neville's last note, which I discovered a few days after his departure or as Mrs. Goddard used to say his ascension, that last note said, "This is my true experience of the Last Supper. Judas betrayed the Messianic secret" so Neville laid claim to absolute understanding of the Lords Supper, the Last Supper because he knew that he had come here to feed with the spiritual word all of those of us who are trapped here in this world of Egypt and this world of Babylon.

Now are there any questions? I've talked for 45 minutes almost. Yes Harry?

Harry: Neville did say the Old Testament foretold what was going to take place [inaudible

00:39:18 - 00:39:42].

Frank Carter: Yes. Sol in Hebrew means asked, past tense of ask. I think I use it one time as asking because it came across clearer, but it means asked in the sense of searching because he was a Jew, zealot Jew and he was searching. Then he had the great experience of

149

the risen Lord on the road to Damascus, that's where he discovered Jesus I am and after that his name was changed to Paul because when he understood that he was the I am then he knew that he was the maker. So, the animal had been transformed in to the God. God the Father.

Yes Harry.

Harry: Have you told about the fall?

Frank Carter: Yes.

Harry: You just lit up at back of you so beautifully it even extended over here **[inaudible 00:40:50]**.

Frank Carter: Yes, burning. Thank you for telling me that.

Harry: And then it stepped away from you.

[00:41:02] [END OF AUDIO]

Frank Carter Lecture 11: Undated

Scripture, Neville and you. I have already explained that scripture, naturally, is a book which exists in the world, in space and in time. We call it the Bible but that book is actually the record of the being you really are. These eternal visions, these eternal scenes, are sealed up within your very being.

At my second lecture a lady, who is here today, had a vision while I was speaking. She told me that she felt that it was an adumbration and she wanted me to comment on it. Now she had the vision, not once but twice. The reason I was so thrilled about her having this vision is that the depths of her soul, of her being, was projecting into the screen of space. This eternal vision, which I was talking about at that very moment and as I told you when I began this word, I really couldn't be sure that I was interpreting right enough. And so here, while I was speaking, the depths of her being have this vision.

Now the vision was of Neville and this was especially uplifting to me because my message is about a man named Neville, who was in history. After he departed, it became clear that this man will reveal the secret to us of the promise that is, that David is your eternal son. This man, who reveal that secret, in history, has his name concealed in Scripture itself because the name Neville, occurs in pun form, in the Hebrew language as the word Naval **[Hebrew language]** and Naval, in Hebrew means skin bag, which is our condition.

You're a skin bag. When you look at the human body, you are looking at the means by which I am in the world. Now you know that this was Neville's teaching, that there is only one being in the world, his name is I am forever. That is your eternal nature but while you're here, you are wearing these garments of skin and the name for that garment, the hidden name for it is Naval **[Hebrew language]** and that was his name.

151

Last week, I spoke about the book. The book which is both in time and space and the book which is you because think about it this way, the bible is God's novel. You hear how close to Neville the word novel is? You could even go further and say that the Bible is Neville's novel. The author wrote this story. Now Paul, for all intents and purposes, was the founder of a Christian religion. If he has not drafted on to the Christian movement, the substance of the mystery schools, that religion, would not have lasted one generation. It would have died out.

Now there is no record of Paul in the ancient world. The only way we know Paul is that we read his words on the page. Now only the most high can read the word and that's you because when you look at the marks on the page, you read the words, the images form in your mind and then you're in eternity because the mind is eternity itself. The human imagination is eternity and yet eternity is contained in this book, this novel. Now Paul is the one who explains all of the mysteries. He doesn't actually explain them, he expounds them.

Now, who is Paul? They admit that they don't know what the name Paul means. Paul, in Hebrew, means maker. Your maker is your husband. It's also, actually the name of a portion of the Hebrew verb itself. So here is Paul, the maker, who is explaining, expounding these mysteries of Christ and the religion. Now last week, I told about Moses leading the children of Israel out of Egypt. Now you know that Egypt is your own body. While Moses was leading them out, God appeared to them, in the form of a cloud. Now when Paul is writing these words, he is writing in the Greek tongue.

When he tells you that God appeared in the form of a cloud, he is saying God appeared in the form Nephele **[Greek language]**. Now you can hear that this, again, is a play on the name Neville because in English we don't say I have to go we say I '*haf*' to go. You have the "v" converting to the "f" sound. So here is Nephele **[Greek language]**. Now elsewhere, at the very beginning of Acts, when the central

152

character, called Jesus, is ascending into hell, his disciples are standing watching the ascension and then we're told a cloud received him from their sight and immediately there appeared two men beside them and they said: "Why stand ye gazing on to heaven? This same Jesus will come, in like manner as ye have seen him go." Now how did he go?

A cloud received him from their sight, a Nephele **[Greek language]**, received him from their sight. Now again, in the Book of Revelation, at the very beginning of the 10th chapter, we are told, an angel came down from heaven, clothed with a cloud. Now you know that an angel is a messenger. A messenger has come, in the function of an ambassador, to deliver a message. So this angel comes down, clothed as a Nephele **[Greek language]**, delivers his message and this angel has a book in his hand and he tells the one, having the vision, to take the book and eat it. That it will be like honey in his mouth but it will be bitter in his belly.

Now elsewhere, in the Old Testament, we're told to eat the book. Now you know of course, on this literal level, that would be sheer nonsense. So obviously the message is spiritual. In the wilderness, when was Moses was leading the children out, the manna appeared and they fed on the manna. Now Paul told us that this manna was spiritual food. In other words, it was the Word of God and that was Neville's theme. He was always preaching the Word of God. Now listen to the description of the manna. Now, remember, this is a parable. The story never took place on earth but it takes place in eternity, when you read the words and when you gather the clues, which put everything in place.

The manna is described as being like a coriander seed and white. Now the word coriander, in the Hebrew language, is gad. It's spelled G-A-D but it is pronounced *'god'*. So here is the play on our English word god. Now that word gad **[Hebrew language]**, which means coriander, comes from the Hebrew word gadad. Now you know that Neville's last name was Goddard but the English don't say

'Goddard', they say 'Goddad.' Neville Goddad. So here, concealed in the words themselves, is the name of the man who came in history and delivered his message. Now if that weren't enough, the coriander seed is described as being white. The word for white, in Hebrew, is Lavan and Lavan read backward, for in our custom of reading from right to left, is naval.

So here in the description of the manna, are the first and last names of this man who came out of history and his message was, "It's all about you." It's a parable. You wrote the book. You are the Elohim [Hebrew language] here in these garments of flesh, in these naval's. You see you're actually called after his name. Now Paul, as I said the name Paul itself means maker, which shows that the maker, the most high, wrote the story when he tells you all the things about himself. In one place he says, "I have become a food." The word for food is naval [Hebrew language], so he's telling you that he became Neville naval [Hebrew language]. In another place he says, "I, Paul, a prisoner of Jesus Christ."

Now that word prisoner, in Hebrew, is asir [Hebrew language] and that comes from the Hebrew word Asar and Asar [Hebrew language] is the ancient Egyptian god of the dead. As I told you earlier in the lecture, Paul took the ancient, secret, teachings of the Mystery Schools, these teachings were thousands and thousands of years old. He took these teaching and buried them in his letters, so that they could not be seen until the one came into history, to activate the story, as it were. Simply a story of the day but then the history comes the man who has the experience and then scripture starts to come alive. So Paul is telling you that he is Asar [Hebrew language] and the story of Asar [Hebrew language] is that he was resurrected from the dead and this is Neville's great message, that he was resurrected from the dead by seeing his son David.

Now there were two captivities. The one captivity was in Egypt

154

There's no record that the Hebrew people were ever there. Nevertheless, we're told that they came out of Egypt. They were lead by this man Moses, they have that experience of being fed by the manna which is our experience. It's a parable for us but there's no record of that captivity. There is another captivity of the Hebrew people. It is known as the Babylonian captivity. They were actually carried away to Babylon and there they remained until Cyrus, the king of Persia, decreed that the people should be released and go back to Jerusalem and build the temple.

Now I'm not talking about history now. This is a parable because that's your condition, that's my condition. The one captivity is the captivity of the body, to be a prisoner here, in this body. The other captivity is the Babylonian captivity which is to be a prisoner of confusion because Babel, in Hebrew, means confusion. All you have to do is look around at the world today and you see mass confusion. If ever there was a need to be delivered out of a captivity, out of confusion, it's today. Now, when the children of Israel are freed to leave Babylon and go back to Jerusalem, their leader is Ezra and Ezra comes from the Hebrew word Asar. You see, everywhere you look in scripture, this mystery of Asar **[Hebrew language]**, the ancient god of the dead, the ancient story of Mystery Schools is buried.

Asar **[Hebrew language]** is their leader. On the way, there is much talk about taking treasure to the temple. Now the word for treasure, in Hebrew is oh-TSAHR **[Hebrew language]. You h**ear another play on Asar **[Hebrew language]**. When they get to Jerusalem, the construction of the temple is begun and the people gather, this is the part I love because it's our tale. The people gather before the Watergate. Now there can't be anyone here who hasn't heard about the Watergate, so in a parable, here are the people, in time and space, before the Watergate. In other words, an event which is very prominent in our world, our experience. They gather before the Watergate and Ezra, who is really Asar **[Hebrew language],** the one who has risen from

155

the dead.

Ezra reads to them, from the book and reveals the meaning of the book. So you see how literally true this is for the human imagination because this is exactly what happened in our experience with Neville. He came, he told us that he had been resurrected from the dead, before that he talk, imagining creates reality for years, showing that the human imagination is really the most high and you can have anything in this world you want, simply imagining it. Then he had this experience of the promise and he began telling that because he felt this was the message he had really been sent to deliver.

Now when Ezra is reading to the people out of the book, he gives the understanding to the word so that they understand the meaning of the book and then they remember the law of Moses and they understand how to interpret that. Now Paul, as I said before, reveals that he is both naval, the food, the skin bag and that he is Asar, the one who fulfills this ancient mystery religion of being resurrected. Now his message, he consistently calls the Gospel of Christ. He was the first one to use the word '*gospel*'. It's a little confusing because in the Bible, in the New Testament, first you have the four gospels than you have the book of Acts and then you have the series of letters, written supposedly to the churches but they're written to you, the reader. Giving you information about this mystery.

Now that word gospel was taken from the Hebrew term, '*good news*' because they were announcing the good news of Christ. Now that mystery was hidden from the ages until Neville came into the world and revealed that. That Gospel of Christ is that you are the eternal father and that when you see your eternal son, David, you have awakened from this dream, from this world of [unintelligible 00:21:17] and you're ready to go back to eternity. Now that word gospel is taken from the Hebrew word bAsar. You can hear another play on *Asar* [Hebrew language] but this time there's '*b*' in front. Now what makes it

156

conclusive is that this word has two meanings. It means both *good news* and it means *flesh*. So here we come right back to the core of the mystery. The word made flesh and this Hebrew word basar means flesh and that is the gospel.

In one of his lectures, the last year, Neville told that Cyrus is actually David, the true man of the Bible **[unintelligitable 00:22:24]** but he did make that statement, that this king Cyrus is David because in Isaiah, in the 45th chapter, we have these words by the Lord, "Cyrus is my shepherd," them, "Thus saith the Lord to Cyrus, his anointed." Now you know that the qualifier for the Messiah or the Christ is to have been anointed and David was the anointed one the Cyrus. So here, again in a parable, this release from captivity in Babylon was activated by Cyrus, by the anointed. You can't get out of Babylon until you see your son David. It's all about you, yet concealed as a mystery.

Allow me to share an experience I've had. In 1973, late summer or early fall, one night I was winding a clock which I had my mother gave to me. It's an antique clock. I thought I was being very careful and as I wound it, the spring gave way and it stopped on ten, the hour ten o'clock. That night, in vision, in a dream Neville appeared to me, lecturing. I was in a group like this, I was in the army and he said, "10 and now you must jump and 10 and now Bethlehem and now you must jump." He did this over and over, saying those words, "10" and those words, Bethlehem." When I got up in the morning, I went to the concordance, which I use. He said, he told us very definitely, in his lectures, that you can not understand scripture if you don't use the concordance. You must use the concordance to find out what these words mean.

So I looked up 10 and at that point I have not heard of the story of the Ancient Mystery Schools about Osiris or, as he's known in Egyptian, Asar, I had not heard that name and I looked up that name but I didn't get anywhere there because it's defined as being a house

157

of David's, death means house, another word for Dave's but I didn't get anywhere there because the word Dave does not appear in Scripture. The only time they used the word Dave in the concordance was to define this word but the word Dave itself does not appear in scripture. Then just a few days later, I was talking with a friend and she happened to mention some book and mentioned the Egyptian mythology and what have you and I said, "Something tells me that I must read these books."

And she said, "Fine." So she leaned them to me and almost immediately when I take out the book, I discovered the story of the raising of Lazarus which appears in the Gospel of John. Now here again, in scripture itself is a concealed form of this ancient story of Mystery Schools. In the story, Asar is laying in mummy form, in a cave and his son Horus goes to the Mountain, the cave and calls to him and says, "Al-Asar come forth." And Al-Asar rose from the dead and came forth. Now in the course of time, Al-Asar took the form *'Al Osiris'* and then finally became Lazarus, who was the one raised by the character of Jesus in the Gospel.

Now on the mummy case. In the reenactment of this ancient mystery, were inscribed the letters K- R-S-T. *'Krst'* and that is where the word Christ comes from. From this ancient Egyptian ritual of resurrection and then it passed into the Greek tongue. So when Paul is talking about the Mystery of Christ and the Gospel of Christ, he was undoubtedly a member of the Mystery Schools and he understood these mysteries that when he said Gospel of Christ, he was saying the *basar* which is a play of Asar, of Christ and basar means flesh.

That's what those four letters meant in Egyptian. The fleshed one, the one who is in flesh. Now as I've said before, this sounds like a ridiculous story. Outrageous but you have to remember that this is the terminology of the mind that built the Great Pyramid. An astonishing mind. This was their way of taking the mystery of the incarnation and presenting it in a vivid form so that it would make an undoubted impression on the mind.

So just summing up, we have the word Nephele which means cloud which is also a play of the name of the man who revealed this mystery to us because if he hadn't come and told the story, none of us would be here today. We wouldn't have found it out by ourselves. This was another mystery of scripture, that scripture would be made literally true as an experience of the human imagination. Now you are the cloud too. Robert Blake, in his poem *Little Boy Lost,* speaks of the cloud of the flesh. That's we, the cloud of flesh here in this world. Think of it this way too, in this world, there is nothing which is such a perfect image for the imagination, as the cloud. The cloud can assume any form and it's a perfect exercise for the imagination to watch these big, puffy clouds above on marvelous summer days and see the shapes, the animals, the people. Perfect exercise for the imagination. **[sound cut 00:31:04]**

[00:31:10][END OF AUDIO]

Summary

While a portion of several lectures were repetitive, Frank obviously knew Neville's work well, and his knowledge of scripture was brilliantly offered, in hopes that you could connect some dots in your mind. Only you the reader can decide if the evidence given was enough to convince you that Neville Goddard was predestined to come into this world of shadows to tell us all, the great mystery of scripture and if you now believe that Neville's death actually fulfilled scripture.

In Nevilles 1954 lecture "The Pruning Shears of revision, Neville wrote this..."When I was a boy of seven, a lady said to me, "I have had a vision concerning you. I'll make it now very, very clear to you--I do not know what it is you are going to do, but I've been shown you will do something that through the centuries after you are gone man will not undo it. I can see it and through the centuries you will grow in stature long after you have gone. And then three men will be mentioned in hundreds of years to come and you will be one of the three when something is discussed that was done for man."

At the time the lecture was written, Neville had yet to receive The Promise in vision and said at the time, he felt his teachings on revision could be what she was speaking of. Could it be, that revision was just a part of what Neville will go down in history for, and possibly the fuller explanation could be that Neville Goddard was one of greatest men to have ever lived because he fulfilled scripture, betrayed the messianic secret by revealing to mankind that all are God, and all are one, and the bible is our own biography? Could the three men who will go down in history be Paul, Blake and Neville? Time will tell.

In closing, I would like to share this, the name Neville means "new town, city", and Goddard means "God" and then I found this, in the book of Revelations 3:22,

"Him that overcommeth will I make a pillar in the temple of my God, and he shall go no more out: and I will write upon him the name of my God, and the name of the city (city and town are the same word in Hebrew) of my God, which is new Jerusalem (Jerusalem means city of God), which cometh down out of heaven from my God: and I will write upon him my new name."

So this verse says, I will write upon him that overcommeth, the name of my God, and that name is new city of God. The name Neville was given at birth.

Liz Baker

FINI

Frank Carter Audios:

http://www.gnosticaudio.com/Frank-Carter

Free Metaphysical Resources:

http://thebookofmirdad.com
http://theiamdiscourses.com
http://asearchforgod.org
http://iammeditations.org
http://christreturns.org
http://pistissophiaaudio.com
http://williamwwalter.com
http://jeshuathepersonalchrist.org
http://www.feelingisthesecret.org
http://www.atyourcommand.org
http://www.awakenedimaginationandthesearch.org
http://www.nevillegoddardfreedomforall.org
http://www.nevillegoddardoutofthisworld.org
http://www.prayertheartofbelieving.com
http://www.nevillegoddardseedtimeandharvest.org
http://www.thelawandthepromise.com
http://www.thepowerofawareness.org
http://www.yourfaithisyourfortune.com
www.NevilleGoddardFreeLectures.Com
http://thenevillegoddardproject.org

www.AudioEnlightenment.Com

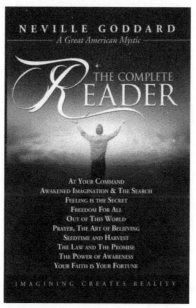

CPSIA information can be obtained
at www.ICGtesting.com
Printed in the USA
LVHW091316080121
676068LV00018B/153